Chinese in Steps

步步高中文

Volume IV

主编：	George X Zhang	张新生
编者：	Linda M Li	李明芳
	George X Zhang	张新生
	William X Yu	俞贤富

CYPRESS BOOKS

Cypress Book Co. UK Ltd.

Chinese in Steps Series
Chinese in Steps Volume Four
By George X Zhang, Linda M Li, William X Yu

Editor: Shurong Zhai, Ranran Du
Cover Design: Wenqing Zhang

First published in Great Britain in April 2009
Reprinted in July 2014

Cypress Book Co. UK Ltd.
Unit 6 Provident Industrial Estate
Pump Lane
Hayes UB3 3NE
02084530687
02085611062 (Fax)
Email: info@cypressbooks.com

Find us at www.cypressbooks.com

ISBN 978-1-84570-0249

Printed in China

Preface

Chinese in Steps is a series of textbooks designed for English-speaking adults who learn Chinese either as part of their degree study at university, or simply as part of their professional or self-development programme. While aiming to deliver an effective and enriching experience in learning the Chinese language, the textbooks also take into consideration the needs of those who seek externally validated qualifications.

Chinese in Steps aims to develop learners' productive communicative competence by focusing on key generic speech patterns and making listening and speaking the core activities of each lesson. As reading skill is crucial for adult learners to acquire in order to use and understand Chinese effectively, the readers' reading and writing skills are developed at the same time. This approach is based upon our cognitive research on how English speaking adults learning Chinese as well as our experience in teaching Chinese to such learners. The layout of the book is designed to make the contents easy to access and follow, for example grammar explanations are given where necessary but grammatical jargon is kept to a minimum.

Chinese in Steps consists of several stages, and there are two books for each stage. The books for the first two stages: Beginners and Lower Intermediate levels. They are designed to cover most key speech patterns, fundamental grammatical knowledge and about 900 of the most frequently used characters. By the end of these two stages, learners should have covered enough ground to be able to cope with many everyday life needs in a Chinese-speaking environment. The contents are also comparable to the current requirements of higher GCSE and up to AS level in the British education system, thus similar to the B1 level of the Common European Framework for languages.

Volume IV of **Chinese in Steps** is the second book of the Lower Intermediate stage and it is recommended for those who have completed Volume III. This volume is designed to review major speech patterns covered so far and to use the language in scenarios that readers are most likely to encounter in China or a Chinese speaking environment. Like the three previous volumes, this book also contains 10 lessons. Each lesson has one or two dialogues and a reading passage usually set in a everyday life scenario but with a more extended vocabulary. The relevant language usages - particularly on the structure of Chinese vocabulary are explained in the notes on grammar and the exercises. Cultural notes still remain, but now an additional reading is included at the end of each lesson introducing a common Chinese proverb and its story. Chinese language learners can expect to encounter many of such proverbs as they continue with their study.

The authors would like to thank many colleagues for their constructive feedback and suggestions, especially PC T'ung and Eun Bahng who gave their inspiration and support in the initial stages of this series. Thanks also go to many teachers and Chinese language learners in the SOAS Language Centre and European Business School London for their support in piloting this book and in providing practical feedback. Finally, we would also like to express our gratitude to Ru Jing and Zhang Wenqing of Cypress Books UK Ltd for their dedication and help in the publication of this textbooks series.

George X Zhang
Linda M Li
William X Yu

November 2008

目 录 Contents

预备课

Learning Objectives
    This lesson revises the essential speech patterns and vocabulary covered in Book Three. It serves as a preparatory lesson for Book Four.

对话 1   **Dialogue One**

学生：师傅，我去北京语言大学。

师傅：好。你的行李这么多，小箱子放在大箱子上，可以吗？

学生：大箱子里面有瓶子，小心别把瓶子弄破了。

师傅：车后备箱恐怕装不下了。

学生：那把小箱子放在我旁边的座位上吧。

师傅：好。上车吧。

学生：谢谢。

师傅：你是来上学的吧？

学生：对，我来学一年中文。

师傅：你是哪国人？

学生：一下子说不清楚。我爸爸是法国人，我妈妈是德国人。

师傅：你是在哪儿出生的？

学生：德国。不过一岁时我就去了法国，我是在法国长大的。

师傅：你是在哪儿上的学？

学生：小学是在法国上的，中学和大学是在英国上的。

师傅：你拿的是哪国护照？

学生：我有两本护照，一本是法国的，一本是英国的。

师傅：那你只能说是欧洲人了。

学生：对，我是欧洲人，西欧人。

对话 2　　　　**Dialogue Two**

学生：师傅，北京的交通总是这么拥挤吗？

师傅：今天还可以，有时候更拥挤。

学生：真没想到北京有这么多汽车，跟伦敦差不多。

师傅：现在有钱的人多了，有汽车的人也就多了。

学生：我听说中国是自行车的王国，上下班时人们都骑自行车。

师傅：那是过去。现在开车的、坐地铁的、坐公共汽车的、坐班车的、打的的、骑自行车的、什么样的都有。

学生：师傅，北京汽车进城要不要交进城费？

师傅：不用。听说伦敦进城要交五镑钱,是吗？

学生：现在涨了，要交八镑了。

师傅：太多了!一天八英镑，合人民币一百多块钱呢。

学生：多是多，可是现在开车上班的人少了，交通好多了。

师傅：出租车司机怎么办？他们天天在城里开车，也要交钱吗？

学生：好像他们不用交。

师傅：这还差不多。

Notes

后备箱	hòubèixiāng	boot (car)
一下子	yíxiàzi	at one go (in a few words)
长	zhǎng	grow, grow up
西欧	Xī'ōu	western Europe
交通	jiāotōng	traffic, communication
拥挤	yōngjǐ	crowded
班车	bānchē	service bus
进城费	jìnchéngfèi	congestion charge (for driving into city)
合	hé	(colloquial) be equivalent to
这还差不多		That's probably reasonable

课文　　　　　　　　Text

画儿是谁偷的?

张先生是个警察。这天晚上，他接到了一个电话，听不清说话人的声音，只听到有人说：美术馆 (art gallery)的名画儿被偷了。他放下电话后马上去了美术馆。美术馆里有两个工作人员，一个是上早班的，一个是上晚班的。张先生问他们：“是谁发现画儿被偷了?”上晚班的说：“他刚才告诉我的。”张先生就问上早班的：“你是什么时候发现画儿被偷走的?”上早班的说：“就在刚才。我两个小时前关门的时候画儿还在。回家的路上我想起来有件东西忘在办公室了，所以又回来了。到了这儿以后，我发现画儿不见了。”这时张先生又问：“你们认为 (think) 画儿是谁偷的呢?”上早班的人说：“不知道是谁打的电话。他一定跟偷画儿的人有关系。”张先生说：“你说得对。我知道是谁偷的了。”

问题:

1. 张先生怎么知道画儿被偷了? *Phone call*

2. 美术馆有几个工作人员? *2*

3. 是谁最先发现画儿被偷了? *Early shift worker*

4. 他们什么时候发现画儿被偷了? *When the early shift worker came back to the office*

5. 上早班的工作人员为什么又回来了? *Left something in the office*

6. 你认为是谁偷的? *Early shift worker - knew about phone call.*

> **口语练习**　　**Speaking Practice**

1. 情景对话：两人一组，一人当出租汽车司机，一人当留学生，在对话中了解以下情况：

kuàng

jiǔ

－ 留学生是哪国人？学了多久的汉语？
－ 留学生想不想住在当地人家里？
－ 留学生想不想天天坐出租车去上学？
－ 留学生想不想租车出去玩儿？他想去哪里玩儿？
－ 出租车司机是老北京吗？他住在市中心吗？
－ 出租汽车司机觉得他的收入怎么样？
－ 北京的交通怎么样？北京的天气怎么样？
－ 出租汽车司机有没有朋友的孩子想学英语？

jiāo tán

2. 你坐飞机去北京，你和坐在你旁边的人交谈。你想知道：

converse

－ 他／她为什么去北京？

zhù duō jiǔ

－ 他／她要在北京住多久？他／她要住在哪儿？
－ 他／她都打算在北京做什么？

zì jǐ

－ 他／她是不是自己一个人去北京？
－ 他／她还打算去中国什么地方？

> **听力练习**　　**Listening Practice**

1. a. 出租车上　　　　b. 机场里　　　　　c. 汽车站里
2. a. 有人偷了　　　　b. 有人拿错了　　　c. 我太累了
3. a. 我的中文书　　　b. 我的护照　　　　c. 一件礼物　　present
4. a. 又生气又着急　　b. 给警察打了电话　c. 告诉了老师
5. a. 系里的老师　　　b. 看门的师傅　　　c. 一个没见过的人
6. a. 护照上　　　　　b. 箱子里面　　　　c. 行李卡上
7. a. 他没吃过西餐　　b. 饭很便宜　　　　c. 他不要我的钱
8. a. 这位好司机　　　b. 司机的老板　　　c. 饭店经理

语法练习   Grammar Practice

单项选择

1. 请告诉我您打算星期几 ____ 中国去。

    a. 想   b. 到   c. 要

2. 旗袍看 ____ 很漂亮，可是大多数人穿不了，只有瘦人才能穿。

    a. 上来   b. 出来   c. 起来

3. 这个人非常聪明，什么东西都学得 ____。

    a. 下   b. 过   c. 了

4. 请你快把行李准备 ____，我们马上就走。

    a. 好   b. 到   c. 了

5. 你能不能写得清楚一点儿，我看不 ____ 这是什么。

    a. 好   b. 懂   c. 了

6. 她人 ____，可是很多人都喜欢她。

    a. 好看   b. 很好   c. 不漂亮

7. 这本书写得不 ____，没有人爱看。

    a. 好极了   b. 怎么样   c. 很不错

8. 你怎么连这么大的字都看不 ____？！

    a. 见   b. 好   c. 完

9. 这么多的饭我们吃不 ____，快给老王送一点儿去。

    a. 好   b. 到   c. 了

10. 她一边说，一边哭。没说几句就说不 ____ 了。

    a. 下去   b. 下来   c. 上来

选词填空

用"着、了、得、就、过、正、到"填空

花园里放 ____ 一张桌子，一只兔子(rabbit)和一个戴 ____ 大帽子的人 ____ 坐在桌子旁边喝茶。桌子下面躺 ____ 一只 ____ 在睡觉的老鼠(mouse)。一只可爱的小松鼠(squirrel) ____ 靠(to lean against)在老鼠身上说话。桌子大 ____ 很，可是他们看 ____ 爱丽丝(Alice)来了，____ 说："没有地

方了，没有地方了！"爱丽丝说 "地方多 ＿＿＿ 很"，就在桌旁坐 ＿＿＿
下来。

兔子说："喝点儿酒吧。"可是桌子上只有茶，没有酒。爱丽丝说：
"我没喝 过 酒，不会喝。"

认字识词　　**Words with Known Characters**

查找出下列词汇的词义，并翻译成英文

名词	动词
形容词	副词
代词	专有名词
数词	量词
介词	连词
感叹词	象声词

翻译练习　　**Translation**

1. May I leave my luggage here?

2. There are too many books and they can't fit into my bag.

3. How much does a ticket to Derby cost?

4. Can you pay my drink for me first?

5. Transport is the biggest problem here.

6. The weather in Shanghai is quite similar to that in London.

7. Your luggage is too heavy and you can't take it onto the airplane.

8. I am always very busy in December and don't even have time to visit my mother.

9. I didn't expect him to be over sixty years old because he looks as if he is in his forties.

10. I am afraid I will have to see your passport before I can give you the ticket.

第三十一课　在学校注册

> Learning Objectives
> How to register for a course/club
> Understanding about studying in China
> How to fill in a course application form in Chinese

生词 1　　New Words

读	dú	动	read, study (a subject)
报到	bàodào	动	report one's arrival or presence
如果	rúguǒ	连	if 如 if; like
学位	xuéwèi	名	(academic) degree
中文系	Zhōngwénxì	名	department of Chinese language and literature
进修	jìnxiū	动/名	engage in advanced studies 修 repair, study
注册	zhùcè	动/名	register 注 record, register 册 volume, book
录取	lùqǔ	动/名	admission; admit (on a programme) 取 get, take
通知书	tōngzhīshū	名	(information) letter, notification
健	jiàn	形	healthy; strength, invigorate
李健	Lǐ Jiàn	专名	Li Jian, Jay Lee
有意思	yǒuyìsi	动/名	be interesting 意思 meaning
起名	qǐmíng	动/名	to name, give name to
力量	lìliàng	名	strength 量 capacity; quantity
填写	tiánxiě	动	fill in (form), write
表格	biǎogé	名	forms 格 square formed by cross lines; check
预订	yùdìng	动	book (a place, ticket etc) in advance 订 book; subscribe
办理	bànlǐ	动	deal with, process 办 do, handle
手续	shǒuxù	名	procedure 续 continue
办公室	bàngōngshì	名	office
交费	jiāo fèi	动	pay fees
钥匙	yàoshi	名	keys 钥 key 匙 spoon

对话 1　　　　Dialogue One

学生：请问，读中文的是在这儿报到吗？

老师：如果你读学位，请到中文系报到。

学生：我不读学位，我是来进修的。

老师：那你找对地方了，进修的就是在这儿登记注册。

学生：谢谢! 这是我的录取通知书和护照。

老师：你的英文名字叫Jay Lee，中文名字叫李健，很有意思。

学生：这个名字是我的中文老师给我起的，我很喜欢。

老师：不错，很有力量。请你填写一下这张表格。

学生：用中文填还是用英文填？

老师：如果你能用中文填，那就用中文填。

学生：好的。老师，我还预订了留学生宿舍。

老师：办理完登记手续以后，到对面的办公室去交费领取钥匙。

学生：谢谢。

生词 2　　　　New Words

王小明	Wáng Xiǎomíng	专名	Wang Xiaoming				
来自	láizì	动/介	come from				
马来西亚	Mǎláixīyà	专名	Malaysia				
理科	lǐkē	名	science (subjects of study)			科	branch, subject
数学	shùxué	名	maths	数	number		
杂志	zázhì	名	magazine	杂	mixed	志	records
阅览室	yuèlǎnshì	名	reading room	阅	read	览	browse
文科	wénkē	名	liberal arts				
设备	shèbèi	名	facilities	设	set up		
先进	xiānjìn	形	advanced				
空调	kōngtiáo	名	air conditioning	调	adjust		
不然	bùrán	连	otherwise, if not				
学习	xuéxí	动	study				
大量	dàliàng	副	a great quantity, a large number				
零起点	língqǐdiǎn	名	zero starting point	起点	starting point		
为	wéi	动	be; become				
一般	yìbān	副/形	ordinary, common; generally			般	type; like
大约	dàyuē	副	approximately	约	about; make an appointment		

补充词汇　　Additional Vocabulary

化学	huàxué	chemistry	政治	zhèngzhì	politics
生物	shēngwù	biology	经济	jīngjì	economics
物理	wùlǐ	physics	教育	jiàoyù	education
地理	dìlǐ	geography	商务	shāngwù	business
心理	xīnlǐ	psychology	建筑	jiànzhù	architecture
历史	lìshǐ	history	法律	fǎlǜ	law

对话 2　　**Dialogue Two**

王小明：你好！我叫王小明，来自马来西亚。

　李健：你好！我叫李健，来自英国。

王小明：我就住在你对面，325 号房间。

　李健：你也是来读语言的吗？

王小明：不，我是来读理科的，我读数学。

　李健：你去过学校的图书馆没有？我想去借本杂志看看。

王小明：学校有文科和理科两个图书馆，我只去过理科图书馆。

　李健：图书馆的设备怎么样？

王小明：很先进，有很多计算机，还有空调。

　李健：阅览室大不大？

王小明：很大。不过人很多，你要早去，不然就没有座位了。

　李健：真的？！那我得走了。回头见。

王小明：回头见。

去中国学习汉语

如果你想去中国学习汉语，你要先找好学校。中国很多大学都开设对外汉语课，有的在汉语系，有的在语言中心。每年都有大量的外国留学生到中国的大学学习汉语。

开始上课以前，你要先参加分班考试。初级班为零起点，一点儿汉语都不会的同学也可以参加。中级班的同学需要掌握八百到一千个汉字，并且能用汉语进行交谈。高级班的同学至少需要认识一千五百个汉字，还要能读懂中文报纸，看懂中文电视节目。初、中、高级班各班人数通常在二十人左右。

中国的学校一般上午八点开始上课，十二点吃午饭，中午休息两个小时，下午两点又开始上课。每周上课的时间大约为二十个小时。中国的大学一年分为两个学期，每年的九月初和二月底开学。每个学期的学习时间为十六到二十周。学校一般都有留学生宿舍，宿舍里面有电视、电话、空调、冰箱等设施，留学生大多喜欢住在校园里。

中国大学的学期

An academic year for most higher education establishments in China consists of about forty calendar weeks, which are usually divided into two semesters running from early September to January with a break of 3 weeks for Chinese New Year, then from February to early July, followed by 8 weeks summer vacation. Unlike in the UK, there is no half term or reading week during the semester in Chinese universities, but instead you have midterm examinations. It is common to have more than 20 contact hours of teaching per week for core modules, with further elective modules available. In addition, there is less course work but more formal examinations than in the UK.

语法注释　　Grammar Notes

1. 如果 -- While such conditional conjunctions are used in Chinese, they are often omitted if relationship is clear from the context. For example:

   (1)（如果）你不去，我也不去。

   If you don't go, I'm not going either.

   (2)（如果）他能做好，谁都能做好。

   If he can do it, anyone can.

   However, if the condition relates to a past subjunctive, the conjunction 如果 is normally included. For example:

   (3) 如果你早点开始学，现在汉语应该说得很流利了。

   If you'd started studying earlier, you would have been fluent by now.

   (4) 如果他们昨天都来帮忙，这工作今天就该做完了。

   If they had all come to help yesterday, the work would have been finished today.

2. 不然就没有座位了。--"Otherwise there is no seat left." 不然 is the same as 不然的话 meaning "otherwise". Both expressions are commonly used in spoken Chinese. 了 suggests an imminent change of the state. For example:

   (1) 你快走吧，不然就晚了。

   Go quickly, otherwise you'll be late.

   (2) 你应该休息两天。不然的话，你会累病的。

   You should rest for a couple of days, otherwise you'll get ill with tiredness.

口语练习　　Speaking Practice

角色扮演

A: 你是一名新生，在校园里遇见了一个学生。你想知道他的个人情况以及学校的宿舍、图书馆和餐厅等的情况。

B: 你是一名老生，你给A介绍一下个人和学校的情况。

听力练习　　Listening Practice

1.	a. 法国	b. 美国	c. 英国
2.	a. 游览北京	b. 在图书馆学习	c. 在家里玩电脑
3.	a. 月票	b. 录取通知书	c. 书包
4.	a. 丢了	b. 没有收到	c. 被朋友拿走了
5.	a. 学费	b. 护照	c. 简历
6.	a. 中文系	b. 音乐系	c. 数学系
7.	a. 不给他注册	b. 查找他的名字	c. 打电话给他的朋友
8.	a. 回家	b. 去找录取通知书	c. 去交钱

语法练习　　Grammar Practice

单项选择

1. ＿＿＿ 我明年去中国，我一定去找你。

   a. 不然　　　　b. 如果　　　　c. 因为

2. 我很幸运，我被上海大学 ＿＿＿ 了。

   a. 报到　　　　b. 通知　　　　c. 录取

3. 我们学校语言中心的设备很 ＿＿＿。

   a. 先进　　　　b. 新鲜　　　　c. 好极了

4. 请问，在哪儿 ＿＿＿ 住宿手续？

   a. 办理　　　　b. 注册　　　　c. 写

5. 李健 ＿＿＿ 一个医生家庭。

      a. 出来　　　　　　b. 是　　　　　　c. 来自

6. 我还没有拿到学位，_____ 这个工作就是我的了。

      a. 不但　　　　　　b. 不然　　　　　　c. 不是

7. 房子是 _____ 人住的，你把房子空着，房子也会坏的。

      a. 需要　　　　　　b. 不要　　　　　　c. 一定

8. 在中国，对着门的座位 _____ 上座。

      a. 办　　　　　　b. 让　　　　　　c. 为

选词填空

用 "可以、报到、和、读、考试、如果、一起、参加、到、然后" 填空

    如果你来我们学院 _____ 学位的话，本科要读四年。申请人要有高中以上学历，汉语水平 _____ 成绩要达到四级以上。你将和中国的本科学生 _____ 上课，不过你可以少选几门选修课。_____ 你是交换学生，你的学分可以转换。

    如果你来我们学院进修的话，你学习一到两年都 _____。你要先到我们的对外汉语系 _____，在那里学习汉语 _____ 中国文化。学生注册后要参加考试，_____ 分班学习。学院共有四种班，入门班、初级班、中级班和高级班，每班八 _____ 十二人。学习期间，学生可以 _____ 汉语水平考试。

认字识词　　　Words with Known Characters

1. 查找出下列词汇的词义，并翻译成英文

总数	注意
画册	杂物
思想	游览
阅读	比如
修理	学科

2. 翻译下列名词，并找出其结构规律

老汉	老虎
老公	老婆
老大	老小
小吃	小费
小店	小菜
小人书	小朋友

3. 请至少再找出五个同样结构的词

翻译练习　　　Translation

1.　The reading room at British Library does not have air conditioning.
2.　Shall we meet at the coffee shop opposite my office at 12 tomorrow?
3.　I can't find your name. Have you booked a room?
4.　Students who are going to study Chinese please go to the second floor to register.
5.　I am from Vietnam, he is from Mali.
6.　You must pay the accommodation fee first, otherwise you can't have the key.

成语故事　　　The Stories Behind Chinese Idioms

井底之蛙

　　一只青蛙（qīngwā）(frog) 住在一口井（jǐng）(well) 里。它高兴时就在井里跳来跳去。天热了，它在水中游上游下，觉得很快乐。它想，我这里又大又舒服，谁也比不上我！

　　一天，青蛙在井边遇见了一只从海里来的大海龟（hǎiguī）(turtle)。青蛙就对海龟说："你看，我住在这里多快乐！你为什么不下来玩玩儿呢？"海龟听了青蛙的话，倒真想进去看看，可是它太大了，进不去。海龟只好趴在井口上对青蛙说："青蛙老弟，你见过大海吗？"青蛙说："大海比我的井大吗，海龟老兄（lǎoxiōng）(elder brother)？"海龟就把大海有多大、多深、多广都跟青蛙讲了，青蛙这才知道，井外还有这么大的天地。

实用练习   **Module Practice**

护照用名	姓		照　片
	名		
国　籍		出生地点	
出生日期	年　　　月　　　日	男 ☐	
		女 ☐	
已婚 ☐	护照号码		宗教
未婚 ☐			
最后学历		现职业	
现工作单位			
永久通讯地址			
电话	传真	E-mail	
目前通讯地址			
电话	传真	E-mail	
申请学习时间	从　年　月　日　到　年　月　日		
现有汉语水平 （词汇量）			
A 无　　　B 大约800　　　C 大约1500　　　D 大约2500　　　E 大约3500			
学生本人签字			
日期			

第三十二课　选修课

Learning Objectives
　　Making choices: the course to take or a club to join
　　Offering a reasoned explanation for your choice
　　Knowing about exercise and health in China

生词 1　　New Words

选修	xuǎnxiū	动/名	select an optional course	选	select
目录	mùlù	名	list, catalogue	目	list; eye
武术	wǔshù	名	martial arts	武	military 术 art
学名	xuémíng	名	scientific name, formal name		
乒乓球	pīngpāngqiú	名	table tennis	乒乓	onomatopoeic characters
活动	huódòng	动/名	exercise; activity	活	live; alive
校队	xiàoduì	名	school/college team	队	team
队员	duìyuán	名	team member		
私人	sīrén	形	private, personal	私	private, personal
教练	jiàoliàn	名	coach, trainer		
商量	shāngliang	动/名	consult, discuss		
门	mén	量	M.W for a subject of study		
学生证	xuéshēngzhèng	名	student card	证	certificate, card; proof
自动	zìdòng	形/副	automatic		
方便	fāngbiàn	形	convenient		

对话 1　　Dialogue One

小李：您好！我想选修中国功夫课，可是目录上没有。

老师：有，你看，在这儿。

小李：武术就是功夫吗？

老师：对，武术是学名。

小李：我明白了，谢谢。

老师：武术课一周一次，星期二下午三点到四点。

小李：星期二下午我有乒乓球活动。

老师：这么巧，你是校队队员吗？

小李：不是，我刚刚开始学，请了个私人教练。

老师：那你跟教练商量一下，看看能不能换个时间。

小李：好。我从小就喜欢中国功夫，我一定要选修这门课。

老师：那你可以现在注册。你带学生证了吗？

小李：我的学生证还没有办好，我还没拍照片呢。

老师：大厅里就有自动照相机，瞧，就在那边！

小李：我看到了，真是太方便了！我现在就去拍。谢谢！

老师：不客气！

◆ **生词 2**　　　　　**New Words**

死	sǐ	形/动	to death (intensifier: "tired to death"); dead, die					
每	měi	代	every, each					
节	jié	量	period, session					
大部分	dàbùfen	名	most of	部	department, part, section			
迟到	chídào	动	arrive late	迟	late			
不好意思	bù hǎo yìsi	形	embarrassed, sorry					
自觉	zìjué	形	self-conscious					
书法	shūfǎ	名	calligraphy					
健身房	jiànshēnfáng	名	gym	健身	keep fit	身	body	
俱乐部	jùlèbù	名	club	俱	all, complete			
锻炼	duànliàn	动	take physical exercise	锻	forge	炼	refine	
不仅	bùjǐn	连	not only	仅	only			
而且	érqiě	连	and, but also	而	but	且	and, just	
不仅…而且…		连	not only…but also…					
棒	bàng	形/名	very good (colloquial); bat, stick					
棒球	bàngqiú	名	baseball					
广场	guǎngchǎng	名	(city) square					
身体	shēntǐ	名	body	体	body			
重要	zhòngyào	形	important					
青年人	qíngniánrén	名	the youth					
改变	gǎibiàn	动	change	改	change, correct			
方式	fāngshì	名	manner, approach	式	manner; style			

◆ **补充词汇**　　　**Additional Vocabulary**

体育馆	tǐyùguǎn	sports hall, stadium	会员费	huìyuánfèi	membership fee
壁球	bìqiú	squash	跑步机	pǎobùjī	treadmill
保龄球	bǎolíngqiú	bowling	划船器	huáchuánqì	rowing machine
手球	shǒuqiú	hand ball	哑铃	yǎlíng	dum bell
棒球	bàngqiú	cricket	运动会	yùndònghuì	sports meeting
球拍	qiúpāi	bat	奥林匹克	Àolínpǐkè	Olympics

对话 2　　　　Dialogue Two

小方：小李，我快要累死了，每周要上18节课。

小李：那我就更不用活了，我要上22节，而且大部分都在上午。

小方：我的也是。天天早上8点就有课。

小李：我已经迟到两次了，真有点不好意思。

小方：问题是这里迟到的人很少，大家都很自觉。

小李：你还选修了别的课吗？

小方：选了，中国书法和太极拳。你呢？

小李：我参加了健身俱乐部，下午我要去健身房锻炼。

小方：学校里有健身房吗？

小李：不仅有，而且很棒。

小方：真的？我还以为中国人只喜欢打乒乓球呢。

小李：他们什么球都喜欢。

小方：是吗？他们好像不喜欢打棒球。

小李：不是不喜欢，而是没有场地。

课文　　　　　　　　　Text

<h2 style="text-align:center">新的生活方式</h2>

　　现在在中国，健身非常流行。男女老少都很喜欢健身。老年人一般喜欢慢跑、打太极拳和跳舞。在城市里，每天早上你都会看到很多老年人到公园去，先慢跑几分钟，然后打打太极拳。夏天的晚上，他们常常来到广场，和朋友们一起跳舞锻炼身体。他们都觉得开始锻炼以后，身体比以前好多了。现在锻炼已经成了他们生活中重要的一部分。

　　最近几年来，在大城市里到处都可以见到健身房，青年人都很喜欢去健身房锻炼。锻炼完以后可以在那里和朋友会面，喝杯咖啡。有的人认为健身是为了锻炼身体，可是有的人认为健身不仅仅是为了锻炼身体，健身还可以改变一个人的生活方式。这是一种新的生活方式。

语法注释　　　　　　　**Grammar Notes**

1. **换个时间** -- "Change to another time." An expression often used when the time offered is not suitable. Please note the use of **个**.

2. **我快要累死了**。 -- "I am almost tired to death." **死** here means "extremely", and it usually follows an adjective to form a colloquial expression of "adj＋**死**＋**了**". For example:

   ⑴ **这两天事情很多，我们都快忙死了**。

   There's been a lot to do this past couple of days, we've been rushed of our feet.

   ⑵ **饭做好了没有，我都快饿死了**。

   Is the food ready? I'm starving to death.

3. **那我就更不用活了**。 -- "Well, my situation is even worse." (lit: "In that case, I have even less chance to survive"). Please note the use of **更**.

4. **不仅…而且…** -- "not only…but also..." The second part of the collection is usually used together with **还** or **也**. In addition, either **不仅** or **而且** may be omitted in many cases. For example:

    (1) **我不仅要选修武术，而且还要选修书法**。

    I not only want to take martial arts, but also calligraphy.

    (2) **王老师（不仅）歌唱得好，而且舞也跳得好**。

    Mrs Wang not only sings very well, but also dances well too.

5. **不是 A 是 B** -- "it is not…but…" The expression is usually to correct an erroneous impression or belief. For example:

    (1) **他不是不能来，而是不想来**。

    It's not that he can't come but that he doesn't want to come.

    (2) **我不是不想唱，而是真的不会唱**。

    It's not that I'm not willing to sing, but that I really can't sing.

中国人的健身活动

Physical exercises are part of Chinese way of life though they take many different forms. Many state institutions still hold annual competitive sports events. For ordinary people, the most popular forms of physical exercises are strolling (slow walking), jogging, taiji and qigong. You will see these activities taking place all around you if you are in urban area of China. Over the last twenty years, dancing (both Chinese and western) has gained enormous popularity in urban areas, especially amongst retired people. For young professionals, gyms and sports clubs seem to be their favourites. In some metropolitan cities, paid gym or health club membership cards are among the most favoured gifts for the young people.

口语练习	**Speaking Practice**

小组活动

1. 一人当健身房注册员，其他人提问题，例如健身房的设施、时间、费用等。

2. 每人介绍一下自己最喜欢的运动。

听力练习	**Listening Practice**

1. a. 机场　　　　　b. 酒吧　　　　　c. 舞会
2. a. 医生　　　　　b. 工程师　　　　c. 教师
3. a. 音乐　　　　　b. 数学　　　　　c. 商务
4. a. 出了事故　　　b. 太累了　　　　c. 没有学生
5. a. 今天晚上　　　b. 明天晚上　　　c. 后天晚上
6. a. 踢足球　　　　b. 打乒乓球　　　c. 打篮球
7. a. 姚明　　　　　b. 李明　　　　　c. 姚英
8. a. 当教练　　　　b. 当老师　　　　c. 打篮球
9. a. 2米　　　　　 b. 2.06米　　　　c. 2.26米
10. a. 3号　　　　　b. 13号　　　　　c. 30号

语法练习	**Grammar Practice**

单项选择

1. 今天晚上我们开会 ＿＿＿ 一下下周的活动，好不好？

   a. 选修　　　　　b. 商量　　　　　c. 做

2. 王先生是我的 ＿＿＿ 马术教练。

   a. 锻练　　　　　b. 私自　　　　　c. 私人

3. 狗子是他的小名，他的 ＿＿＿ 叫贵生。

   a. 学名　　　　　b. 姓名　　　　　c. 真名

4. 他 ＿＿＿ 会打羽毛球，而且还会打棒球。

   a. 不是　　　　　b. 不仅　　　　　c. 不喜欢

5. _____ 意思，我今天又迟到了。

    a. 不好　　　　　　b. 真有　　　　　　c. 没有

6. 如果我不在家，我家的电话会 _____ 转 (transfer) 到我的手机上。
^{zhuǎn}

    a. 自行　　　　　　b. 应该　　　　　　c. 自动

7. 你想 _____ 我，我还想改变你呢！

    a. 改变　　　　　　b. 变化　　　　　　c. 修改

8. 我家附近没有地铁站，进城很不 _____。

    a. 快　　　　　　　b. 方便　　　　　　c. 便宜

选词填空

用"感觉、种、平地、差不多、爱好者、就像、那儿、一开始"填空

    北京附近有好几个滑草场，夏天你可以去 _____ 滑草健身。滑草场的经理说，来滑草的有三 _____ 人：一种人是滑雪 _____ ，到了夏天没有地方去，就来滑草。另一种人不敢滑雪，就来滑草，试试滑雪是什么 _____ 。还有一种人就是喜欢户外运动的人，他们喜欢滑草场的蓝天绿草。滑草跟滑雪 _____ ，要穿滑草器，也要用滑草杖。_____ 和走路差不多，慢慢滑起来 _____ 滑雪一样，可以滑得很快。人们可以在山坡上滑，也可以在 _____ 上滑。

> 认字识词　　　**Words with Known Characters**

1. 查找出下列词汇的词义，并翻译成英文

        选美　　　　　　干活

        私自　　　　　　自私

        武打　　　　　　目前

        活鱼　　　　　　死人

        队长　　　　　　证人

2. 翻译下列名词，并找出其结构规律

男子	演员
脑子	卫生员
篮子	警卫员
读者	科学家
记者	歌唱家
作者	数学家

3. 请至少再找出5个同样结构的词

翻译练习　　　　Translation

1. He was late again yesterday, but he did not seem to feel embarrassed at all.

2. My girl friend has not only started to go to the gym every day, but has also hired a personal trainer.

3. Table tennis is a very popular sport in China. Most universities have a team.

4. It is not that he did not want to eat, but that he couldn't eat because of his illness.

5. Chinese calligraphy is very beautiful but seems difficult to learn. Do you think I can learn it?

6. When can we register for the *Kongfu* class? I have been interested in this since childhood .

成语故事　　　The Stories Behind Chinese Idioms

bá　　　miáozhùzhǎng
拔 (pull) 苗 助 长
　　　　　dàomiáo

　　从前有一个农夫 (farmer)，种 (plant)了稻苗 (rice seedling) 以后希望能早早
　　　　　　　　　　　　　　　　　　　　　　tián
有收成 (harvest)。因此，他每天都跑到稻田 (rice paddy)去看。

　　到了稻田以后，他发现稻苗长得非常慢。他心想："怎样才能让稻苗长
得又快又高呢？"他想了又想，最后终于想出了一个好方法，就是把稻苗拔
高一点儿。

　　xīnláo
他辛劳 (work hard)了几天，然后高兴地对家里人说："这几天真把我累坏

了，我都帮助稻苗长高了很多！" 他儿子<u>赶快</u>（hurriedly）跑到地里一看，稻苗全都<u>枯死</u>（wither）了。

实用练习　　Module Practice

　　你每星期一、三、五上午和星期二下午有必修课，现在你还需要选修五门选修课。请根据你的具体情况，从下表中选出五门课作为你的选修课。此外，请写一篇250字的文章，说明你为什么选修这五门课。

选修课课程表

	星期一	星期二	星期三	星期四	星期五
8:00—9:50	语法	语音	商务汉语	中国文学	中国音乐
10:10—12:00	中国文化	中国经济	汉字	写作	书法
2:00—3:50	书法	中国文学	武术	商务汉语	语法
4:00—5:50	写作	太极拳	语音	中国文化	中国电影
4:00—5:50	汉字	中国舞蹈	气功	中国经济	武术
6:30—7:50	中国音乐	中国电影	中国舞蹈	太极拳	气功

第三十三课　在银行

Learning Objectives

Opening a bank account / applying for a credit card in China

Expressing feelings of good fortune

Understanding the banking industry in China

生词 1　　　New Words

职员	zhíyuán	名	clerk, employee	职	profession
账户	zhànghù	名	account	账	account
往来账户	wǎnglái zhànghù	动	current account	往	toward
身份证	shēnfènzhèng	名	ID card 身份 identity, status	份	share
奖学金	jiǎngxuéjīn	名	scholarship	奖	reward
存	cún	动	deposit		
活期	huóqī	名	current (account)		
利息	lìxī	名	interest (rate)		
比较	bǐjiào	副/动	relatively; compare	较	compared with; comparably
另外	lìngwài	副	besides	另	other, another
死期	sǐqī	名	fixed term (deposit account)		
定期	dìngqī	名	fixed term		
联系	liánxì	动	contact	联	connect
信用卡	xìnyòngkǎ	名	credit card	信用	credit
不管	bùguǎn	连	no matter	管	mind; manage
国际	guójì	名	international	际	border, boundary
货币	huòbì	名	currency	货	commodity, goods
结算	jiésuàn	名	account settlement		
香港	Xiānggǎng	专名	Hong Kong	香 fragrant	港 harbour
港币	Gǎngbì	专名	Hong Kong dollar		

对话 1   **Dialogue One**

大卫：你好！我想开一个普通的往来账户。

职员：带身份证了没有？

大卫：我没有身份证，我带了护照。

职员：护照也可以。你有奖学金吗？

大卫：我不是学生，我在这儿工作。

职员：对不起。你在哪个公司工作？

大卫：可口可乐公司。

职员：你每月打算存多少钱？

大卫：两万块左右。

职员：活期账户利息比较低，你另外再开一个定期账户吧。

大卫：什么是活期，什么是定期？

职员：活期就是往来账户，定期就是死期账户。

大卫：我先开一个活期账户，过几天再来开一个定期账户。

职员：好！请填一下这张表，把地址和联系电话写清楚。

大卫：另外，我想问一下，外国人可以申请信用卡吗？

职员：不管是外国人还是中国人，都可以在这里申请信用卡。
　　　我们有长城人民币信用卡和长城国际信用卡。

大卫：国际信用卡以什么货币结算？

职员：美元和港币两种。

大卫：我申请一个以美元结算的长城国际信用卡。

职员：好！请你再填一张表，请好好看一下说明再填。

◇ **生词 2**　　　　**New Words**

丢	diū	动	lose		
地址	dìzhǐ	名	address	址 site	
单元	dānyuán	名	unit, module	单 single; bill	元 unit
密码	mìmǎ	名	pin number		密 secret
超市	chāoshì	名	supermarket		
放心	fàngxīn	形	rest assure of		
盗用	dàoyòng	动	embezzle	盗 steal	
旧	jiù	形	old (not for age)		
住处	zhùchù	名	dwelling	处 place; department	
名列	míngliè	动	list as	列 rank	
系列	xìliè	名	series; serial		
品种	pǐnzhǒng	名	kind, type		
借记卡	jièjìkǎ	名	debit card		
透支	tòuzhī	动	overdraft	透 permeate, transparent	支 pay
使用	shǐyòng	动	utilise, use		
标记	biāojì	名	mark	标 mark	

◇ **补充词汇**　　**Additional Vocabulary**

账号	zhànghào	account number
结余	jiéyú	account balance
贷款	dàikuǎn	loan
汇票	huìpiào	bill for remittance
维萨卡	Wéisàkǎ	Visa (card)
对账单	duìzhàngdān	statement
自动取款机	zìdòng qǔkuǎnjī	cash dispenser
建设银行	Jiànshè Yínháng	Bank of Construction
农业银行	Nóngyè Yínháng	Agriculture Bank
交通银行	Jiāotōng Yínháng	Bank of Communications
工商银行	Gōngshāng Yínháng	Industrial and Commercial Bank of China
进出口银行	Jìn-chūkǒu Yínháng	Bank of Import and Export

对话 2　　　**Dialogue Two**

小方：你好，我的信用卡丢了。

职员：你的卡号是多少？

小方：00359486721。

职员：姓名？

小方：方英。

职员：地址？

小方：香港路25号，9号楼2单元1号。

职员：你的信用卡密码是多少？

小方：我记不清了，好像是"1225"。

职员：不是数字。

小方：哦，想起来了，是"南京"。

职员：对了，你最后一次使用信用卡是在什么时候，什么地方？

小方：今天中午，在超市里。我买了六十多块钱的东西。

职员：请放心，你的卡没被盗用。

小方：谢天谢地！

职员：你的旧卡已被停用，新卡很快就会寄到你的住处。

小方：谢谢你的帮助。

中国银行信用卡

中国银行是中国最重要的银行之一。2005年中国银行在英国《银行家》杂志评选出的"世界1000家大银行"中名列第18位。

中国银行的长城信用卡系列深受人们的喜爱。长城信用卡品种包括长城电子借记卡、长城人民币信用卡普通卡、长城人民币信用卡照片金卡、长城人民币信用卡金卡、长城国际信用卡普通卡和长城国际信用卡金卡。

在中国申请信用卡，你除了要有工作以外，你的账户里还要有现金。申请长城人民币信用卡普通卡时，你的账户里最少得有1000元人民币，你可以最高透支5000元。透支期，也就是信用期，为60天。你可以在标有中国银行长城信用卡标记的商店、饭店、酒楼、机场、医院等场所，使用长城信用卡结账。使用长城信用卡每年需交纳20元的手续费。

中国的银行业

The banking industry has been going through drastic changes since the introduction of the open door policy in China. With China's accession to the WTO, the Chinese banking industry is being opened up to the outside world and foreign banks can deal in RMB business transactions now. All the major Chinese commercial banks have been restructured. As a result, business operations in most Chinese banks have become increasingly similar to those of foreign commercial banks. The Bank of China used to be the only bank dealing in foreign currencies, but nowadays, all the major Chinese commercial banks provide services in both local and foreign currencies.

语法注释　　Grammar Notes

1. **不管是外国人还是中国人，都可以在这里申请信用卡。**

   -- "Everyone can apply the credit card here, no matter Chinese or foreigner."

   不管...都... is a construction with a sense of concession. **还是** is used to indicate alternative conditions. For example:

   (1) **不管是他来,还是他太太来,还是他女儿来，我们都十分欢迎。**

   No matter whether he, his wife or his daughter comes, we'll still welcome them.

   (2) **不管他来还是不来，我们都应该准时** (on time) **开始。**

   Regardless of whether he comes or not, we should still start on time.

   不管... can also be used to indicate the inclusiveness.

   (3) **不管下不下雨，我都会在大门口等你。**

   Whether it's raining or not, I'll still be waiting for you in the main entrance.

   (4) **不管他怎么说，我们都应该准时开始。**

   Regardless of what he says, we should still start on time.

2. **谢天谢地！** -- A phrase to express a sense of feeling relieved or fortunate about something. For example:

   (1) **谢天谢地！你们都来了，我还以为你们都忘了呢。**

   Thank heavens you've come, I thought you'd all forgotten.

   (2) **谢天谢地！我这次考试考得不错，九月可以去中国了。**

   Thank goodness I've done OK in these exams and can go to China in September.

3. **我申请一个以美元结算的国际信用卡。** -- "I apply to settle an international credit card in dollars." **以...结算：** to settle an account or a transaction in a nominated currency or a form of currency.

口语练习　　Speaking Practice

角色扮演

1. A: 你刚到北京，去银行开一个新账户。

   B: 你是银行职员，你给A开账户。

2. A: 你的信用卡被偷了，你打电话去银行说明情况。

   B: 你是银行职员，你接听A的电话，为A的信用卡办理停用。

听力练习　　Listening Practice

1. a.王府井　　　　b.天安门　　　　c.北京大学
2. a.带现金　　　　b.电汇　　　　　c.带旅行支票
3. a.找服务员　　　b.离开了　　　　c.一边看书一边排队
4. a.他是外国人　　b.他要取外汇　　c.他要取人民币
5. a.英镑　　　　　b.美元　　　　　c.人民币
6. a.要等一个星期　b.他账户里没有钱　c.他没带护照
7. a.换钱表　　　　b.取钱表　　　　c.申请密码表
8. a.银行关门了　　b.他忘了密码　　c.支行里没钱

语法练习　　Grammar Practice

单项选择

1. 我们可以用人民币 ＿＿＿ 吗？

   a.打算　　　　　b.总算　　　　　c.结算

2. ＿＿＿ 信用卡都需要什么证件？

   a.请求　　　　　b.申请　　　　　c.申要

3. 老王的行李箱打不开了，因为他把 ＿＿＿ 忘了。

   a.密码　　　　　b.密号　　　　　c.密数

4. ＿＿＿ 是白猫还是黑猫，能抓住老鼠，就是好猫。
   _{lǎoshǔ}

   a.不管　　　　　b.虽然　　　　　c.不仅

5. 不知道怎么搞的，我的电话号码被 ＿＿＿＿ 了。

    a. 使用   b. 盗用   c. 偷盗

6. 我学汉语是想 ＿＿＿＿ 一名翻译。

    a. 成为   b. 是   c. 当成

7. 小李在汉语口语比赛中 ＿＿＿＿ 第二。

    a. 列名   b. 当成   c. 名列

8. 我想开一个人民币帐户，＿＿＿＿ 再开一个美元帐户。

    a. 而且   b. 另外   c. 不过

选词填空

用"了、多少、过、最高的、先进、站着、进口、当时"填空

      昨天上午我和我的同学到 ＿＿＿＿ 上海，下午，我们到南京路去买东西。十年前，我和我的父母亲来 ＿＿＿＿ 上海，我记得上海是一座漂亮的古城（ancient city），当时，并没有 ＿＿＿＿ 高楼。黄河路上的国际饭店只有24层，可已是 ＿＿＿＿ 最有名的高楼了。十年后的今天，上海到处都是高楼，＿＿＿＿ 有88层。当年的国际饭店还在那里 ＿＿＿＿，可是成了一个小弟弟。上海现在也有了地铁，上海的地铁比伦敦的还漂亮、还 ＿＿＿＿。上海商店里的东西真多，有中国制造的，也有从国外 ＿＿＿＿ 的。人们高高兴兴地选择（select）他们心爱（favourite）的商品。

> **认字识词**   **Words with Known Characters**

1. 查找出下列词汇的词义，并翻译成英文

        管理   管家

        账本   算账

        奖金   丢面子

        提货单   寄存处

        香水   香米

2. 翻译下列词汇 ，并找出其结构规律

道路	喜爱
数量	变化
歌唱	城市
光亮	生产
表格	等候
偷盗	存放

3. 请至少再找出5个同样结构的词

翻译练习　　Translation

1. No matter whether he goes or not, we shall go tomorrow anyway.

2. Thank goodness my wallet didn't go missing. I nearly stopped my credit card.

3. Credit cards nowadays all require a pin number.

4. If you want to apply for this job, you need to fill in the form and send it to that company.

5. There are a lot of people in Hong Kong. Buildings there are usually tall and rooms are comparatively small.

6. It is really convenient to use a cash machine to withdraw money. You can get it whenever you want.

成语故事　　The Stories Behind Chinese Idioms

画蛇添足
huàshétiānzú

楚国有个人赏 (bestowed on) 给他手下的人一壶 (pot) 酒。这壶酒如果大家一起喝是不够 (enough) 的。于是，大家商量决定，每个人在地上画一条蛇，谁先画好就把这壶酒给谁喝。

有个人画得很快，不一会儿蛇就画好了。他拿起酒壶刚要喝，回头一看，别人都还没有画好，他便给蛇添 (add) 起脚来。正在这时候，另外一个人也画好了。那人马上夺过酒壶说："蛇本来没有脚，你为什么要给它画脚呢？这壶酒该我喝。" 说完，他咕嘟(glug)咕嘟把酒喝光了。

> 咕嘟
> gūdū

实用练习　　　Module Practice

银行网页

以下是一家中国银行的网址主页。你的朋友想知道怎样开一个活期的人民币帐户，他/她应该查看哪个/些标题？如果他/她想要开信用卡呢？

银行风貌	个人金融	银 行 卡	金融咨询	网上论坛	商城	理财	保险
人才招聘	企业金融	机构业务	投资银行	资产托管	基金	外汇	股票
资产处置	电子银行	网上银行	电话银行	手机银行	黄金	债券	北京

第三十四课　在邮局

Learning Objectives
How to post a parcel in a post office
Specifying essential conditions
Understanding the Chinese lunar calendar

生词 1　　　New Words

包裹	bāoguǒ	名	parcel	裹 wrap
绣花	xiùhuā	名/动	embroidery; embroidered	绣 embroider
睡衣	shuìyī	名	pyjamas, nightdress	
被套	bèitào	名	quilt cover	被 quilt　套 cover（量）a set of
床单	chuángdān	名	bedsheet	单 sheet
按照	ànzhào	代	according to	按 by
规定	guīdìng	名/动	regulations; stipulate	规 rule
必须	bìxū	情动	must	必 have to 须 must
检查	jiǎnchá	动/名	inspect; check	检 inspect
手工	shǒugōng	名	handicraft, handmade	
制品	zhìpǐn	名	products	
奶奶	nǎinai	名	grandma	
海运	hǎiyùn	名	transport by sea, surface mail	运 transport
空运	kōngyùn	名	transport by air, airmail	
称	chēng	动	weigh, be called as, scale	
纪念	jìniàn	名/动	commemorate	纪 record; discipline 念 study, read
邮票	yóupiào	名	(postage) stamp	邮 post
属	shǔ	动	be born in the year of , belong to	

对话 1　　**Dialogue One**

学生：你好！我寄一个包裹。

职员：里面是什么东西？

学生：一件绣花睡衣、一个绣花被套和一条床单。

职员：按照规定，我必须打开检查一下。

学生：检查吧，没问题！

职员：看来你很喜欢中国的手工绣花制品。

学生：不是我，是我奶奶喜欢。她一定要我买一些寄回去。

职员：你寄哪儿？

学生：马德里。

职员：是海运还是空运？

学生：空运。我想让她早点收到。

职员：好！称一下吧。

学生：对了，我还想买几张纪念邮票。

职员：今年是猪年，我们有猪年纪念邮票。

学生：太好了！我是属猪的，我买十套。

生词 2　　　　New Words

邮局	yóujú	名	post office	局	bureau
阴历	yīnlì	名	Chinese lunar calendar		
阳历	yánglì	名	solar calendar, Gregorian calendar	阳	Sun, masculine
历法	lìfǎ	名	calendar, calendrical method		
相差	xiāngchà	动	differ from each other	相	each other
月份	yuèfèn	名	month		
当年	dàngnián	名	at that time (year)		
属相	shǔxiàng	名	zodiac sign		
比如	bǐrú	动	for example		
原来	yuánlái	副	in fact, actually, originally	原	original
到底	dàodǐ	副	ultimately, in the end		
用户	yònghù	名	user, customer		
或	huò	连	or		
轮船	lúnchuán	名	ship steamer	轮	wheel
运输	yùnshū	名/动	transport	输	transport, lose
平常	píngcháng	形	ordinary, common	平	even, level
挂号	guàhào	名/动	registered; register		
查询	cháxún	动	ask, seek information	询	ask
保价	bǎojià	名	value insurance	价	value, price
赔偿	péicháng	动	compensate　赔 compensate　偿 repay, pay back		

补充词汇　　Additional Vocabulary

鼠	shǔ	mouse, rat	鸟	niǎo	bird
虎	hǔ	tiger	鹅	é	goose
兔	tù	rabbit, hare	鸡	jī	cock
蛇	shé	snake	狼	láng	wolf
羊	yáng	sheep/goat	狐狸	húli	fox
猴	hóu	monkey	狮子	shīzi	lion

对话 2　　　　**Dialogue Two**

小王：小李，猪年的纪念邮票出来了，你看，漂亮吧？！

小李：真漂亮！

小王：你不是也属猪吗？快去邮局买一套吧？！

小李：我不属猪，我属狗。

小王：怎么会呢？！我们都是1983年出生的。

小李：可我的生日是阳历1月，那时阴历还是1982年12月呢。

小王：阴历和阳历是怎么回事？我不太懂。

小李：阳历是西方人使用的历法，阴历是中国人使用的历法。

小王：为什么会有两种不同的历法？

小李：因为我们是以太阳来计算日期的，而中国人是以月亮来计算的。

小王：我明白了。那阴历和阳历相差几天？

小李：一个多月。

小王：所以一月份出生的人不一定属当年的属相。

小李：不仅仅是一月份，二月初出生的人也不一定，比如说小方。

小王：怪不得小方的床头上挂着一只小狗，原来她也是属狗的。

课文　　　　　　Text

怎样在中国寄邮件

如果你去邮局寄邮件，邮局的职员会问你是寄航空邮件、水陆路邮件还是空运水陆路邮件。到底哪一种方法好呢？

应该说各有各的好处。航空邮件时间快，一般一个星期左右就可以收到，所以虽然邮费较贵，很多用户还是喜欢使用这种邮寄方式。水陆路邮件是使用汽车、火车或轮船来运输的，时间比较长，可是邮费比较便宜。空运水陆路邮件是使用国际航班、汽车、火车或轮船来邮寄的。时间上比航空邮件慢，比水陆路邮件快；邮费上比航空邮件便宜，比水陆路邮件贵，是用户常用的邮寄方式。

邮局里的服务员还会问你是寄平常邮件、挂号邮件还是保价邮件。寄平常邮件寄丢了也没有办法查询，所以如果是贵重的邮件，一定要寄挂号。如果你寄的是包裹，那是可以查询的。但是如果你没有保价，丢失了还是得不到赔偿，因此你最好寄保价。

中国人的属相

There are twelve animals in the Chinese zodiac signs. They correspond to each of the Earthly Branches that forms part of the naming system of the Chinese lunar calendar. These animal signs follow a strict order as listed below and the cycle is twelve years. Since they are calculated according to the lunar calendar, the starting point of each animal year is Chinese New Year, also known as Spring Festival. So if 2000 was the year of Dragon, can you work out which animal year you were born in?

The 12 animals are: rat, ox, tiger, hare, dragon, snake, horse, sheep, monkey, cock, dog, hog.

语法注释　　　**Grammar Notes**

1. **几张** -- 几 means several here, and refers to an indefinite number under ten; like a numeral it goes before a measure word. For example:

   (1) **秋天北京的天气很好，我想在北京多住几天。**

   The weather in Beijing is very good in autumn; I'm thinking of staying for a few more days.

   (2) **那天晚上很冷，酒吧里只有几个人。**

   It was very cold that evening and there were only a few people in the bar.

2. **按照规定** -- according to regulations. For example:

   (1) **按照学校的规定，你必须在九月一号以前注册。**

   According to college regulations, you must register before the first of September.

   (2) **我们已经按照你的要求，把信寄到她的公司去了。**

   In accordance with your requirements we have already sent the letter to her company.

3. **阴历** and **阳历**

   -- There are 3 different calendrical systems in the world, the Gregorian Calendar (**阳历**) which is based on the sun; the lunar calendar (**阴历**) which is based on the Moon; the traditional Chinese calendar (**农历** nónglì — agricultural calendar) which is calculated in association with the movement of the Moon, thus mistakenly called **阴历**. Both the **阳历** and **阴历** are used in China now. The **阳历** is used for most day to day activities, but all Chinese traditional holidays are calculated according to the lunar calendar, so are most auspicious dates for events such as a wedding or the opening of a business. Traditionally, the name of each year repeats itself in a cycle of 60 years as it consists of a combination of two characters, one from the 10 Heavenly Stems (**天干**) and the other from the 12 Earthly Branches (**地支**).

口语练习   **Speaking Practice**

角色扮演

A: 你想寄个生日礼物，但不知道怎么寄，也不知道用哪种方式邮寄好。

B: 你是邮局职员，你告诉A怎么寄，用哪种方式寄最好。

听力练习   **Listening Practice**

1. a. 领带   b. 睡衣   c. 明信片
2. a. 我们欢迎你   b. 北京欢迎你   c. 中国欢迎你
3. a. 她妹妹要两套   b. 她要两套   c. 她和妹妹一人一套
4. a. 旗袍   b. 绣花睡衣   c. 床单
5. a. 睡衣   b. 明信片   c. 中国画儿
6. a. 包   b. 信封   c. 箱子
7. a. 水   b. 药   c. 酒
8. a. 背疼   b. 腿疼   c. 牙疼
9. a. 不能空运   b. 便宜   c. 快
10. a. 保险   b. 包装   c. 保密

语法练习   **Grammar Practice**

单项选择

1. 按照学校的 ＿＿＿，你必须选修五门课。

   a. 规定   b. 一定   c. 需要

2. 张先生有一套熊猫 ＿＿＿ 邮票。

   a. 记录   b. 几年   c. 纪念

3. 星期天大家都喜欢出去玩儿，马路上 ＿＿＿ 都是人。

   a. 到处   b. 到来   c. 走来

4. 我十二点前 ＿＿＿ 赶到火车站，十二点以后就没有车了。

   a. 必要   b. 不必   c. 必须

5. 在我们这儿，有些东西是不能邮寄的，＿＿＿ 狗和猫。

     a. 不比　　　　　　**b**. 比如　　　　　c. 如果

6. 真没想到 ＿＿＿ 你我是校友。

     a. 原来　　　　　　b. 本来　　　　　c. 和

7. 属龙的和属猪的 ＿＿＿ 几岁？

     a. 不到　　　　　　b. 相差　　　　　c. 差不多

8. 李英 ＿＿＿ 是美国人还是加拿大人？

     a. 到底　　　　　　b. 到来　　　　　c. 要是

选词填空

用"使用、到、一般、中间、只有、小月、如、又"填空

    历法 ＿＿＿ 分为三类：太阴历、太阳历和阴阳历。太阴历和太阳历 ＿＿＿ 简称为阴历、阳历。中国 ＿＿＿ 的农历(nónglì)，一般人把它叫做阴历，这是不对的，农历其实是阴阳历。农历每个月初一都正好是月亮在太阳和地球 ＿＿＿，农历的一个月是从新月出现的那一天 ＿＿＿ 下一个新月出现的前一天。农历的大月是三十天，＿＿＿ 是二十九天。因此，农历和阳历不同，农历的大小月不固定(gùdìng)。＿＿＿ 春节的前一天常称为大年三十，但有时候如二零零零年的农历十二月就 ＿＿＿ 二十九天。

认字识词　　　　**Words with Known Characters**

1. 查找出下列词汇的词义，并翻译成英文

       按时　　　　　准时

       念书　　　　　价格

       阳光　　　　　月光

       邮电局　　　　警察局

       问询处　　　　办事处

2. 翻译下列词汇，并找出其结构规律

始终	长短
阴阳	是非
老少	冷热
真假	死活
来往	文武
早晚	轻重

3. 请至少再找出5个同样结构的词

翻译练习　　Translation

1. According to the regulations, you can't bring meat products into the country.

2. I would like to buy some Beijing commemorative stamps.

3. I was born in 1985, do you know which Chinese zodiac animal I am?

4. I used to eat meat, but my doctor told me I'd better eat more vegetables and fruit, so I have not eaten meat since.

5. Why is the parcel I sent in China last month not here yet?

6. How did you post your parcel？ By air or by sea?

成语故事　　The Stories Behind Chinese Idioms

shǒuzhūdàitù
守株待兔

宋(sòng)国有个农夫，有一天，他正在田里干活。突然从远处跑来一只兔子，一下子撞(zhuàng) (bump into) 在稻田(dàotián) (paddy field) 旁边的大树上，当场就倒地死了。农夫看到之后，赶快跑过去把死兔子捡(jiǎn) (pick) 起来，开心地带回家吃了。从此以后，这个农夫天天坐在大树旁，等着兔子再来撞树。他等啊等，可是他不仅没有捡到兔子，连兔子的影子也没见着！农夫的那几块地，却因为太久没有耕种(gēngzhòng) (cultivated)，都荒芜(huāngwú) (weed-filled) 了。

实用练习　　Module Practice

你在邮局寄包裹，试填下列两张表格。

国 内 普 通 包 裹 详 情 单　通知单联

	收件人		
	详细地址：		
	姓名：　　　　电话：		

内装何物及数量

接收局号码：

收寄人员名章

	寄件人	是否保价	重量：　　　克
	详细地址：		单价：　　元/千克
		是□　　否□	挂号费：　　元
	姓名：　　电话：	保价金额：　　元	保价费：　　元
	用户代码：　邮政编码：	备注：	回执费：　　元
			资费：　　元

寄件人声明：同意并遵守背面的"使用须知"，如包裹无法投递，按如下选择处理，请□退还寄件人、□抛弃处理。

签字：_____　　　　　　检查人员名章：_____

① 投递局存　一式四份，请用力填写

国 内 快 递 包 裹 详 情 单　通知单联

	收件人		
	详细地址：		
	姓名：　　　电话：		

内装何物及数量

接收局号码：

收寄人员名章

	寄件人	是否保价	重量：　　克
	详细地址：		挂号费：　　元
		是□　　否□	保价费：　　元
	姓名：　　电话：	保价金额：　　元	回执费：　　元
	用户代码：　邮政编码：	备注：	资费：　　元

寄件人声明：同意并遵守背面的"使用须知"，如包裹无法投递，按如下选择处理，请□退还寄件人、□抛弃处理。

签字：_____　　　　　　检查人员名章：_____

第三十五课 在理发店

Learning Objectives

Getting your hair styled and commenting on appearance;

Using the verbal construction V + 起来;

Learning about the modifier + key word construction

生词 1　　　　　　New Words

发型	fàxíng	名	hair style	发 hair	型	style, shape, model
理发店	lǐfàdiàn	名	hairdressing salon		理发	hair cut
市中心	shìzhōngxīn	名	city centre			
发廊	fàláng	名	hair salon		廊	corridor, veranda
剪	jiǎn	动	cut			
吹	chuī	动	blow dry			
连剪带吹	liánjiǎn dàichuī		cut and blow dry (hair)			
女士	nǚshì	名	lady		士	person
美发	měifà	动/名	have hair styled			
烫发	tàngfà	动	perm one's hair		烫	scald, burn
染发	rǎnfà	动	colour, dye hair		染	(to) dye
东单	Dōngdān	专名	a shopping street in Beijing			
打听	dǎting	动	ask, make an enquiry			

对话 1　　　　Dialogue One

小方：小王，你去哪儿了？我到处找你。

小王：我去邮局了，你找我有事吗？

小方：你的发型不错，我想问问你是在哪家理发店理的。

小王：我是在市中心的一家理发店理的。

小方：那家店叫什么名字？

小王：新新发廊。

小方：贵不贵？

小王：不贵，连剪带吹一共才三十块。

小方：那里有没有女士美发部？

小王：有，那里不仅理发和剪发，而且还烫发和染发。

小方：太好了！我女朋友要染发，我们可以一起去了。

小王：这家理发店很忙，你最好早点儿去。

小方：理发店几点开门？

小王：八点。

小方：你有这家理发店的地址吗？

小王：没有，理发店就在东单，你下车后打听一下就知道了。

生词 2   New Words

排队	pái duì	动	queue	排	queue, row
轮	lún	动/名	become one's turns; turn, wheel		
显眼	xiǎnyǎn	形	conspicuous	显	reveal, show
引起	yǐnqǐ	动	attract, give rise to	引	guide
注意	zhùyì	动/名	pay attention; attention, notice		
短	duǎn	形	short		
板寸	bǎncùn	名	cropped hair	板 plank	寸 Chinese inch
平头	píngtóu	名	cropped hair		
帅	shuài	形	smart, handsome		
精神	jīngshen	动/名	smart looking; lively	精 smart	神 spirit, god
该	gāi	代	this, that, the one in question		
开业	kāiyè	动/名	start up (business)		
于	yú	介	at, in, a surname		
老字号	lǎozìhào	名	long established business		
业务	yèwù	名	business		
出色	chūsè	形	outstanding		
特级	tèjí	形	special grade; class, top class		
美容师	měiróngshī	名	beautician	美容 beauty treatment, make-up	
位于	wèiyú	动	situated at/in		
王府井	Wángfǔjǐng	专名	a shopping street in Beijing	府mansion	井well
大街	dàjiē	名	avenue, main street	街 street	
西单	Xīdān	专名	a shopping street in Beijing		
宾	bīn	名	guest, customer		
航天员	hángtiānyuán	名	astronaut	航天 aerospace	
顾客	gùkè	名	customer	顾 visit, see	
之一	zhī yī		one of	之 of; object substitute	
美白	Měibái	专名	Meibai (a name of hairdresser's shop)		
四联	Sìlián	专名	Silian (a name of hairdresser's shop)		

补充词汇   Additional Vocabulary

洗发液/水	xǐfàyè/shuǐ	shampoo	卷发器	juǎnfàqì	curler
洗发香波	xǐfà xiāngbō	shampoo	吹风机	chuīfēngjī	hair dryer
护发素	hùfàsù	conditioner	理发推子	lǐfà tuīzi	hair clippers
发乳	fàrǔ	hair cream	电动推子	diàndòng tuīzi	electric clippers
发胶	fàjiāo	hair spray	剪子	jiǎnzi	scissors
冷烫液	lěngtàngyè	perming lotion	梳子	shūzi	comb

对话 2　　　**Dialogue Two**

理发员：你们好，请进。

小方：你好。啊，这么多人排队！

理发员：我们这儿有十几位师傅，一会儿就轮到你了。请坐。

小方：谢谢。我们需要拿一个号吗？

理发员：我来帮你拿，这位小姐也是来美发的吗？

小李：对，我想把头发染成黑色的。

理发员：好。不过你的金发很漂亮，染成黑色真可惜。

小李：我的金发在这儿太显眼了。我不想引起人们的注意。

小方：我想理一个短发，可我不知道那叫什么发型。

理发员：那叫板寸，也就是平头。你理板寸一定很帅。

小李：我早就想让他换个发型，短发看起来很精神。

小方：洗起来也方便。

理发员：没错儿。又精神又方便，而且很适合你的脸型。

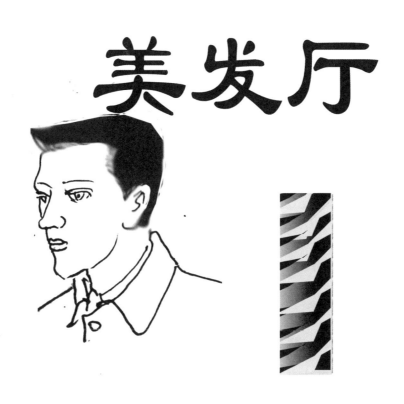

课文　　　　　　　Text

北京的理发店

　　北京市很大，有几百个理发店，有名的理发店也有几十个。王府井大街的美白美发厅就是有名的理发店之一。该店开业于1928年，是北京的一家老字号，当时叫美白理发馆。因为美容已经成为美白主要的业务，所以现在改名为美白理发厅。美白有很多出色的理发师和美容师，仅特级理发师就有三人。

　　四联美发美容公司也位于王府井大街上，是"2000年中国最好的美发美容院"之一。四联设有"女宾理发"、"男宾理发"、"美容室"、男宾美发"贵宾厅"和女宾美发"名人室"。

　　北京人最爱板寸，这种发型老中青都适合。理板寸每人才30元，又便宜又好看。北京的金板寸理发店专理板寸，非常有名。中国很多航天员都是这里的顾客。

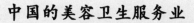

中国的美容卫生服务业

Services involving beauty and hygiene in China have changed dramatically over the last few decades, especially in urban areas and cosmopolitan cities. Most of these services, excluding beauty treatment were in existence before, but the nature and scope of the services were limited. There were public bathhouses, but care was mostly restricted to hair and feet (including pedicure). New beauty services have emerged as a result of much improved standards of living as well as changed lifestyles among younger generations. Today it is not uncommon to see young women having beauty treatment in beauty salons (which usually also do hair).

语法注释　　　　Grammar Notes

1. **连吹带剪** -- 连...带... is a set construction linking two items. For example:

   ⑴ **那家饭店不贵，昨天我们五个人连吃带喝才花了一百英镑。**

   That restaurant is not dear. Yesterday it came to less than £100 for five of us including both food and drinks.

(2) 他们玩得很高兴，连喝带唱一直玩到晚上十二点才休息。

They had a good time, drinking and singing till twelve o'clock at night before they went to bed.

2. 你理板寸一定很帅。 -- If you had your hair cut short, you would definitely look smart. In Chinese, conjunction such as 如果 can often be omitted. The full sentence is 如果你理板寸，（看上去）一定很帅。

3. 看起来 and 洗起来 -- 起来as a complement one sense of 起来 is "start to", "when one comes to". 看起来 has become a set phrase, meaning "look" or "seem". In 洗起来，起来has the sense "when you come to wash it". For example:

(1) 说起来容易，做起来就难了。

It's easy to say but hard to do.

(2) 这菜看起来不怎么样，可吃起来很不错。

This dish doesn't look much but it's delicious when you come to eat it.

4. 没错儿。 -- a colloquial expression particularly popular in Beijing meaning "Right!", "Absolutely!" when agreeing with others.

5. "十几"和"几十"的用法。 --几 is used as an unspecified number between 1 and 9 to indicate an imprecise amount, like "several" in English. Hence, 十几 refers to a number between eleven and nineteen, similar to "a dozen or so" in English, while 几十 means somewhere between ten and one hundred, similar to "dozens" in English. Note while you can say 十几 or 几十, you can only say 几百 "hundreds"or 几千 "thousands"，not the other way round. Remember to use measure word as these are numbers. For example:

(1) 我昨天花了十几块钱打的去学校上课。

Yesterday we spent over ten kuai taking a taxi to college to attend class.

(2) 大门口站着几十个人，男的女的都有。

There are several dozen people standing at the main entrance, both men and women.

口语练习　　Speaking Practice

角色扮演

A: 你去理发店或美容厅理发或美发。你告诉理发师上次做得不好，你希望这次理发师能按照你的想法做。

B: 你是理发师，你想法让顾客满意。

听力练习　　Listening Practice

1. a.他穿新衣服了　　b.他换发型了　　c.他瘦了
2. a.他不喜欢小王　　b.他的头发太长了　　c.他的头发太短了
3. a.想变帅　　b.剪短发便宜　　c.短发方便
4. a.理发师的错　　b.小李的错　　c.明星的错
5. a.黑色　　b.黄色　　c.红色
6. a.小李　　b.理发师们都说　　c.那个理发师
7. a.经理不在　　b.给他剪头的就是经理　　c.不想找经理
8. a.他朋友的妹妹　　b.他妹妹　　c.经理的妹妹

语法练习　　Grammar Practice

单项选择

1. 我家在伦敦的南 ____，三区。

   a.边　　　b.部　　　c.方

2. 短发看起来很 ____。

   a.精神　　　b.精力　　　c.精美

3. 他的发型 ____ 了大家的注意。

   a.形成　　　b.引起　　　c.引出

4. 我没有 ____ 他是什么时候走的。

   a.意思　　　b.注视　　　c.注意

5. 大家都穿校服，你一个人穿便服，你不觉得太 ____ 了吗?

　　a. 精神　　　　　　b. 帅　　　　　　c. 显眼

6. 你对教学工作还很不熟悉，应该好好提高 ____ 水平。

　　a. 服务　　　　　　b. 业务　　　　　　c. 家务

7. 老钱的太太在 ____ 店工作。

　　a. 理发　　　　　　b. 剪发　　　　　　c. 发型

8. ____ 们先生们，谢谢你们来参加今天的晚会。

　　a. 女人　　　　　　b. 女子　　　　　　c. 女士

选词填空

用"再、按照、起来、虽然、正在、而是、可以、还是、顾客、让"填空

　　路易斯（Louis）走进了车站理发馆，他想 ____ 车站的理发师给他理个发。他家就在车站附近，这里除了车站理发馆以外，____ 没有别的理发馆了。路易斯对理发师说："现在店里没有 ____，能不能给我理理发。"理发师说："非常抱歉，____ 规定，我只能为手里有车票的顾客服务。"路易斯没办法，只好买了一张火车票。可是理发师 ____ 不给他理发。理发师说："我们这儿是为坐火车的顾客服务的。____ 你买了车票，可是你没有坐车啊！"路易斯非常生气，大叫____。这时候理发师拿起了电话，打完电话后他对路易斯说："好了，你 ____ 理发了。"路易斯高兴极了，可是理发师说："不是在这儿，____ 在下一站。下一站的理发师 ____ 等着给你理发呢！"

▷ **认字识词**　　　**Words with Known Characters**

1. 查找出下列词汇的词义，并翻译成英文

　　　　护士　　　　　　走廊

　　　　明显　　　　　　英寸

　　　　洗钱　　　　　　照顾

　　　　洗礼　　　　　　宾馆

　　　　染色体　　　　　井井有条

2. 翻译下列词汇 ，并找出其结构规律

黑板	明文
红牌	黄牌
美酒	香菜
怪话	短路
平地	冷盘
空位	旧车

3. 请至少再找出5个同样结构的词

翻译练习　　　Translation

1. I like short hair, as it is very easy to wash.

2. Hair tinting and curling are very cheap there. It would not cost more than £50 altogether.

3. He seems a bit angry. I know that he hasn't had a break for over a month now.

4. London is situated in the South-east of the England, it is not very far from the sea.

5. Mr Wang is a top-class barber, he cuts hair extremely well.

6. There are many people in the queue, it will take a couple of hours before it is your turn.

成语故事　　　The Stories Behind Chinese Idioms

掩耳盗铃
yǎn'ěrdàolíng

　　春秋战国时期有一个小偷，他看中了一只钟，想把它偷走。可是钟太笨重了，他很难搬走。他就找来了一把锤子（chuí），想把钟敲碎（qiāosuì）(break up) 了再搬走。可是他一敲下去，钟就发出了巨大（jùdà）(huge) 的响声。他怕人们听到响声来抓（zhuā）(seize) 他，就把自己的耳朵捂（wǔ）(cover) 上了再敲。他想既然我离得这么近都听不见，其他人当然更听不见了。当然别人还是听到了钟声，小偷被抓住了。

实用练习　　**Module Practice**

　　下面是一个理发店的服务价目表。请写一封电子邮件预定理发时间。你要说明你是谁；你要理什么样的发型；想什么时候去理等等。你还可以问问理发店收不收信用卡；理发店门口有没有地铁站等。

天天理发店价目表

男士剪发		女士美发	
理光头	10元	剪短发	20元
理长发	15元	剪长发	25元
理板寸	20元	洗头	10元
洗头	10元	吹风	15元
吹风	10元	染发	30元
染发	25元	烫发	50元

营业时间：上午8：00 — 晚上9：00

为避免 (avoid) 长时间排队等待，请打电话或发电子信件预约(make an appointment)。

第三十六课　请假

Learning Objectives

Asking someone to pass on a sick leave message;

Writing a short note asking for leave;

Learning about the verb - object construction.

生词 1　　　　　New Words

羊肉	yángròu	名	lamb	羊 goat, sheep
拉肚子	lādùzi	动/名	have diarrhoea	拉 pull; pooh
新鲜	xīnxiān	形	fresh	
熟	shóu/shú	形	cooked	
请假	qǐngjià	动/名	ask for leave	
请假条	qǐngjià tiáo	名	written request for leave/absence	条 note
替	tì	动/介	for, on behalf of	
现成	xiànchéng	形	ready-made	
例子	lìzi	名	example	例 instance
抄	chāo	动	copy	
签	qiān	动	sign	
自己	zìjǐ	代	oneself	己 oneself
原因	yuányīn	名	cause, reason	
相同	xiāngtóng	形	the same	同 identical
笨	bèn	形	stupid, slow	
方法	fāngfǎ	名	method	
聪明	cōngming	形	intelligent, clever	聪 clever

对话 1　　**Dialogue One**

小王：小李，快起床，上课要迟到了！

小李：我今天不舒服，不能去上课了。

小王：你怎么啦？哪儿不舒服？

小李：我昨晚吃了些烤羊肉，没想到拉起肚子来了。

小王：是不是羊肉不新鲜了？

小李：谁知道呢！也可能是没有烤熟。

小王：要不要去医院看看？

小李：不用了，我已经吃了药。

小王：那你好好休息，我帮你请假。

小李：我给老师写个请假条吧。

小王：你能写吗？要不要我替你写？

小李：不用，我自己能写。哎，你知道怎么用中文写请假条吗？

小王：书上有现成的例子，抄一个签上自己的名字就行了。

小李：那怎么行！请假的原因不可能相同啊！

小王：你真笨，你把头疼改成拉肚子就行了。

小李：这是个好方法！还是你聪明。

生词 2　　　　New Words

通知	tōngzhī	名/动	notice	
关于	guānyú	介	about	
讲座	jiǎngzuò	名	open lecture	讲 talk
通告	tōnggào	名	public notice, announcement	
不同	bùtóng	形	different	
更加	gèngjiā	副	even more	
正式	zhèngshì	形	formal	
范围	fànwéi	名	scope, range	范 limits　围 all round
对内	duì nèi	介宾结构	internal	内 inner
对外	duì wài	介宾结构	external	
内部	nèibù	名	internal, interior	
公开	gōngkāi	形	public, open	
广告	guǎnggào	名	advertisement	告 tell
区别	qūbié	名	difference	区 area, zone
商业	shāngyè	名	commercial, business	
告诉	gàosu	动	tell	诉 tell
事先	shìxiān	副	beforehand, in advance	
口头	kǒutóu	形	oral	
书面	shūmiàn	形	written	
紧急	jǐnjí	形	urgent	紧 tight　急 pressing
字样	zìyàng	名	written expressions	
尊敬	zūnjìng	形/动	Dear (addressing letter) respected	尊 respect　敬 honour
准假	zhǔn jià	动	authorize leave; absence	准 allow
敬礼	jìnglǐ	名/动	yours sincerely (ending letter), salutations	
将	jiāng	副	will, about to, be going to	
就业	jiùyè	名/动	to get a job; obtain employment	
就座	jiùzuò	动	be seated, take seat	
学生会	xuéshēnghuì	名	student union	

补充词汇　　Additional Vocabulary

嗓子疼	sǎngzi téng	sore throat	肺炎	fèiyán	pneumonia
腿疼	tuǐ téng	pain in leg	胃炎	wèiyán	gastritis
腰疼	yāo téng	back pain	皮炎	píyán	dermatitis
骨折	gǔzhé	fracture (bone)	过敏	guòmǐn	allergy; allergic
腿断了	tuǐ duàn le	broken leg	心脏病	xīnzàngbìng	heart disease
脚崴了	jiǎo wǎi le	sprained ankle	高血压	gāoxuèyā	high blood pressure

对话 2　　Dialogue Two

小王：小李，你在写什么？

小李：我在写通知。

小王：是关于什么的通知？

小李：音乐讲座的。

小王：你知道通知和通告有什么不同吗？

小李：都差不多，不过通告比通知更加正式一点儿。

小王：通告是不是比通知更大一点儿？

小李：就范围而言，对。因为通知大多是对内的，通告是对外的。

小王：怪不得我经常听人说这是内部通知，不公开。

小李：没错儿。

小王：可以说通告就是公开的通知吗？

小李：可以这么说。

小王：哎，你还知道通告和广告的区别吗？

小李：广告就是广而告之的意思，是为商业服务的。电视上天天都有。

小王：那公告呢？

小李：就是公开告诉你呀！

课文　　　　　　Text

怎样写请假条和通知

当你有急事不能去上班或者上课时，你需要写张请假条请假。写请假条一般不写地址，但必须写清楚收假条的人是谁、请假的人是谁、请假的原因、请假多长时间和写请假条的时间。

如果你有活动需要事先告诉参加的人员，你可以用两种方式通知。一种方式是口头告诉他们，这叫做口头通知。另一种方式是用文字告诉他们，这叫做书面通知。写书面通知要写清楚时间、地点、事情和参加人员，最后要写上发通知的单位和日期。你还可以在"通知"前面加上"重要"、"紧急"等字样，以引起人们的注意。请看下例。

请假条

尊敬的黄老师：

　　今天我病了，拉肚子，不能来上课了，非常抱歉。请求老师准假一天。

　　此致

敬礼

你的学生　李贵
十月十六日

通知

　　五月四日星期三下午，商学院的于院长将来我校作关于就业问题的专题讲座。讲座将于下午两点正式开始，请同学们于两点以前到五号楼二层大教室就座。

学生会
四月二十二日

病假和事假

As elsewhere, if you fall sick and can't go to work in China, you are expected to submit a sick note from a doctor either before or after the absence. In schools a note from parents or at university a note from students themselves (who are adults after all) will do for a short absence for a day or two. In addition, there is another type of leave, similar to unpaid leave in Britain, which is sometimes called "leave of absence" (事假) or leave approved on compassionate grounds. It is usually approved when the applicant has a specific reason , often personal. However, taking such leave could affect the performance assessment of the individual concerned.

语法注释　　Grammar Notes

1. 没想到… -- didn't expect that… For example:

(1) 我没想到他会来。

　I didn't expect that he would come.

2. 谁知道呢！ -- Who knows! This is an expression used to convey a sense of uncertainty on the part of the speaker, often with 呢 at the end. It often implies that the speaker is not in a position to help or is not very keen on the subject being discussed.

3. 要不要我替你写？ -- 替…V… "for" or "on behalf of" someone do something.

For example:

(1) 他现在太忙，我替他去吧？

He's too busy at present, shall I go instead of him?

(2) 我有点感冒，你能替我买点药吗？

I've got a touch of flu, can you buy some medicine for me?

4. 就范围而言 -- 就…而言 is a phrase meaning "in terms of" or "as far as…is

concerned". It is a formal way to draw the listener's attention to an item the speaker

would like to stress. For example:

⑴ 就我而言，我觉得他这么说没什么。

Personally speaking I don't have any problem with him saying that.

⑵ 就这件事而言，我们都认为是你的不对。

As far as this matter is concerned, we all feel you are in the wrong.

5. 广而告之 -- "make known widely". This is based on a Classical Chinese construction.

而 (and) is a function word linking clauses, while 之 (it) usually functions as an

object substitute for something referred to earlier on.

口语练习　　　Speaking Practice

小组活动

A: 你有事不能去参加一个事先定好的活动。你请一位同学把你的情况转告

(inform, pass on information) 大家；

B: 你把A请假的原因转告给C；

C: 你转告给D……N；

N: 你把A请假的原因告诉大家。

大家看看他说得对不对。如果不对，找出是谁把话传错了？

听力练习　　　Listening Practice

1. a. 他有病 　　　　b. 他很忙 　　　　c. 他是一半中国人

2. a. 读书 　　　　　b. 锻炼身体 　　　　c. 看电视

3. a. 八点 　　　　　b. 九点 　　　　　c. 十点

4. a. 他病了 　　　　b. 他要看球赛 　　　c. 他没有做完作业

5. a. 他拉肚子了 　　b. 他头疼 　　　　c. 他妈妈来了

6. a. 在医院里 　　　b. 在家里 　　　　c. 在学校里

7.　a.他头疼　　　　　b.他腿疼　　　　　c.他感冒了

8.　a.他打电话给老师　　b.老师给他打电话　　c.王为给他打电话

语法练习　　　Grammar Practice

单项选择

1.　他做了坏事，你怎么还 ＿＿＿＿ 他说话？

　　a.给　　　　　　　　b.关于　　　　　　　c.替

2.　他今天为什么没有来？你知道 ＿＿＿＿ 吗？

　　a.原本　　　　　　　b.原因　　　　　　　c.原来

3.　今天晚上开会，你 ＿＿＿＿ 她了吗？

　　a.通知　　　　　　　b.通告　　　　　　　c.通报

4.　这两种字体没有什么 ＿＿＿＿。

　　a.区分　　　　　　　b.区别　　　　　　　c.地区

5.　情况很 ＿＿＿＿，你们必须马上出发。

　　a.重要　　　　　　　b.紧急　　　　　　　c.紧要

6.　我们应该 ＿＿＿＿ 老人，爱护孩子。

　　a.尊敬　　　　　　　b.尊重　　　　　　　c.爱护

7.　我弟弟从小就很 ＿＿＿＿，不管什么东西，他都一学就会。

　　a.听话　　　　　　　b.懂事　　　　　　　c.聪明

8.　这儿的空气不 ＿＿＿＿，你应该出去走走。

　　a.新鲜　　　　　　　b.清楚　　　　　　　c.干净

选词填空

用"本来、不管、关于、出去、只好、容易、正式、范围、非常、以为"填空

　　昨天下午，学校里有一个 ＿＿＿＿ 太空的讲座，请了中国第一个太空人杨利伟来讲演。这个讲座 ＿＿＿＿ 只对内，不对外，＿＿＿＿ 是航天系的高年级学生和老师。可是秘书小王搞错了，＿＿＿＿ 是对外开放，他把通告贴了 ＿＿＿＿。

通告一贴出，很多人早早就来到了大教室就座。讲座应该在六点半 ＿＿＿ 开始，可是五点半就已经没有座位了。秘书好不 ＿＿＿ 才给到会的几位老专家找到了座位。航天系的学生 ＿＿＿ 站着听了。可是 ＿＿＿ 是坐着还是站着，大家都热情高涨，这次讲座 ＿＿＿ 成功。

认字识词　　　Words with Known Characters

1. 查找出下列词汇的词义，并翻译成英文

办法	同事
内科	外科
笨蛋	地区
签证	拉面
笨头笨脑	笨手笨脚

2. 翻译下列词汇，并找出其结构规律

倒茶	洗车
经商	扫地
越级	种菜
打字	放羊
打鱼	生孩子
放火	讲话

3. 请至少再找出5个同样结构的词

翻译练习　　　Translation

1. I don't feel well, can you write a sick note for me?

2. None of us expected that he wouldn't speak Chinese.

3. My mobile phone is flat; I never thought yours would be flat as well. How can we find someone to help us?

4. As far as population is concerned, China is the most populous country in the world.

5. – Why is Xiao Wang so formally dressed today?

   – Who knows! He's been quite odd recently.

6. I went to Xinjiang (新疆) in the summer and the roast lamb there was really delicious.

成语故事　　The Stories Behind Chinese Idioms

杯弓蛇影
bēigóngshéyǐng

　　从前有个叫乐广的人请朋友到家里喝酒。可是那位朋友喝完酒回家后就生病了。乐广派人去问候他，才知道他怀疑酒杯里有条小蛇。酒杯里怎么会有蛇呢？经过仔细观察 (observation)，乐广终于 (finally) 找到了原因。他再次把那位朋友请到家里，还让他坐在上次喝酒的位子上。乐广给朋友倒了一杯酒，一条小蛇又在杯中出现了。这时候乐广把挂在墙上的弓 (bow) 取下来，杯中的小蛇也就不见了。原来挂在墙上的弓的影子倒映 (reflected) 在酒杯里，看起来很像一条小蛇。他朋友的病也立刻好了。

实用练习　　Module Practice

1. 下个月底学生会要举行新年舞会，请你写一个通知告诉大家。
2. 写一个请假条，请假的原因请自己找。

第三十七课　写信

Learning Objectives

Talking about differences and similarities

Reading and writing Chinese letters

Learning about adverb + verb/adjective construction

生词 1　　New Words

退	tuì	动	send back, return, retreat	
信封	xìnfēng	名	envelope	封 seal; M.W for letter
反	fǎn	形	opposite; against	
相反	xiāngfǎn	形	opposite, contrary	
啦	la	助	a phrase-final particle (fusion of le + a)	
难道	nándào	副	surely not, do you mean to say	
靠	kào	介/动	keep to, rely on	
不见得	bújiàndé	副	not necessarily	
例外	lìwài	名	exception	
阿拉伯	Ālābó	专名	Arab, Arabic	阿 noun prefix 伯 uncle
表达	biǎodá	动/名	express	达 reach
日期	rìqī	名	date	
辫子	biànzi	名	plaits, pigtail	辫 plaits
袍子	páozi	名	robe, gown	
世界	shìjiè	名	world	世 world　界 boundary
多元	duōyuán	形	multiple, diversified	元 element, component

对话　　　　　　　Dialogue

小张：小李，你寄的信给退回来了。

小李：怎么回事？

小张：信封的格式不对，你把地址写反了。

小李：写反了？难道是寄信人地址在下，收信人地址在上？

小张：当然啦！

小李：怎么中国这儿什么都是相反的？！

小张：那不见得。

小李：你看，中国开车靠右行，英国开车靠左行。

小张：大部分国家都是靠右行，只有少数几个国家例外。

小李：中国人姓在前，名在后。

小张：阿拉伯国家也是这样。

小李：中国人表达日期从大到小，西方人是从小到大。

小张：日本人就是从大到小的。

小李：中国男人穿裙子，留辫子。

小张：真的，我怎么没看见？！你是在哪儿看见的？

小李：在电影里。

小张：我说呢。不过那不是裙子，那是袍子。

小李：那留辫子是怎么回事？

小张：现在不是有很多男人留辫子吗？世界是多元的。

生词 2　　　　New Words

亲爱的	qīn'ài de		dear (intimate form of address), darling 亲 next of kin; kiss
一切	yíqiè	代	everything, all　　切 be suitable, be close to
挂念	guàniàn	动	worry about, concern
语音	yǔyīn	名	pronunciation
语调	yǔdiào	名	intonation　　　调 intonation, tone
错误	cuòwù	名	mistake, error　　误 error
收获	shōuhuò	名	gains, harvest　　获 capture, reap
全部	quánbù	副	completely　　　全 whole, complete
讲课	jiǎng kè	动	give lecture, teach
一开始	yìkāishǐ		at the beginning
吃力	chīlì	形	strenuous, require great effort
习惯	xíguàn	动/名	get used to; habit 惯 spoil; be used to
居住	jūzhù	名/动	habitation; live　居 live
条件	tiáojiàn	名	conditions
同学	tóngxué	名	classmate, schoolmate
食物	shíwù	名	food　　　　　食 food; eat
狗不理包子	Gǒubùlǐ bāozi		a well known brand of steamed dumpling in Tianjin
附上	fùshàng	动	attach　　　　附 add, attach
好客	hàokè	形	be hospitable　好 like, love
伙伴	huǒbàn	名	partner　　伙 mate　伴 companion
于爱华	Yú Àihuá	专名	a name
误以为	wù yǐwéi		mistaken for; mistakenly believe
如此	rúcǐ	副	be like this; so, such
祝	zhù	动	wish
健康	jiànkāng	形	healthy　　　　康 health

课文　　　　　　　　　Text

亲爱的高老师：

　　您好！时间过得真快。我们来中国已经一个月了。这里的一切都很好，请不要挂念。我们现在每周上18个小时的课。我们有六七门课，我最喜欢的是口语课和语法课，你知道我的语音语调不太好，语法的错误也很多，上这两门课我的收获很大。这里的老师全部都用汉语讲课。一开始我感到非常吃力，现在我已经习惯了。

　　我现在住在学校的留学生宿舍里，这里的居住条件非常好，跟大饭店差不多。房间里有电视和空调，每天还有服务员来打扫房间。我都给惯坏了。学校的餐厅也很不错，不过北京的食物非常便宜，我常常和同学出去吃饭。我很喜欢吃烤鸭和狗不理包子。

　　来北京前您告诉我们北京又大又漂亮，可是我没有想到北京有这么大，这么漂亮！附上几张照片，这是我和李健在校园里拍的。我们还没有好好出去玩过。

　　中国人很好客，我已经交了不少朋友。我还有一个语言伙伴，她叫于爱华，是英语系的学生。很多人误以为她是我女朋友。不过我倒是希望如此，因为她人很好，长得又非常漂亮。关于她，我有很多要对您说的，今天就写到这儿吧。我还要准备明天的听写呢。

　　等着您的回信。

　　祝您身体健康！

您的学生: 王京

2006.3.15

语法注释　　　　Grammar Notes

1. **那留辫子是怎么回事？** -- **怎么回事** "how come?" "what's it all about?" is a colloquial expression asking for the details or reasons, possibly with a sense of emphasis. For example:

    (1) **你腰疼是怎么回事？**

    How come you have backache?

    (2) **你昨天没去上班，怎么回事？**

    How come you didn't go to work yesterday?

2. **我们还没有好好出去玩过。** -- **好好** means "really" or "properly" here, but it also has a more literal meaning of "nicely". For example:

    (1) **这本书你要好好（地）看一下。**

    You should take a proper look at this book.

    (2) **这件事你得好好地跟他说。**

    You must talk to him properly about this.

3. **告诉、说、讲** -- note the differences between them in terms of usage as below:

    (1) **他告诉我老王去北京了。**

    He told me old Wang had gone to Beijing.

    (2) **他说老王去北京了。**

    He said old Wang had gone to Beijing.

    (3) **她讲课时说老王去北京了。**

    When she was teaching she said old Wang had gone to Beijing.

4. **希望如此。** -- It is a common expression, meaning "I hope so".

狗不理包子

狗不理包子 is a well known brand of steamed bun with stuffing originating in Tianjin, though the name of the brand doesn't sound very elegant. The story goes like this. Over a hundred years ago, there was a young boy nicknamed 狗不理 by his parents because of his strong character. 狗不理 literally means that even dogs take no notice. But the boy later turned out to be a master chef for making 包子 which were really delicious. Due to his nickname, his 包子 were referred to as 狗不理包子 and the name soon travelled far beyond the city of Tianjin. It was said that the Empress Dowager Tzu-hsi (慈禧太后) liked 狗不理包子 so much that she ordered more to be sent to her after she had a taste of them.

口语练习　　Speaking Practice

小组活动

1. 介绍你们国家写信和写信封的格式。
2. 介绍你们国家开车和穿衣的习惯。
3. 介绍你们国家和别的国家非常不同的习惯。

听力练习　　Listening Practice

1. a. 他们是律师	b. 他们是中文老师	c. 他们是工人
2. a. 山东	b. 山西	c. 广东
3. a. 以为他脑子坏了	b. 以为他感冒了	c. 以为他被人卖了
4. a. 马、茶	b. 吗、草	c. 妈、菜
5. a. 包裹	b. 明信片	c. 信
6. a. 他自己	b. 朋友王京	c. 他的妈妈

7. a. 寄信人地址在上　　　b. 收信人地址在下　　　　c. 收信人地址在上

8. a. 地址写反了　　　　　b. 没有邮票　　　　　　　c. 邮票价钱不对

语法练习　　　Grammar Practice

单项选择

1. 在这时候，我很难用语言 ＿＿＿ 我的感情。

　　a. 表示　　　　　　b. 表现　　　　　　c. 表达

2. 他 ＿＿＿ 比你高多少。

　　a. 不怎么　　　　　b. 不由得　　　　　c. 不见得

3. 这个星期很忙，大家都得来上班，谁也不 ＿＿＿＿!

　　a. 里外　　　　　　b. 例外　　　　　　c. 除外

4. 他们以为圣诞节可以好好休息一下，结果正好 ＿＿＿，他们的经理
　　叫他们圣诞节加班。

　　a. 相当　　　　　　b. 相近　　　　　　c. 相反

5. 在信里，他给他妈妈 ＿＿＿ 了几张自己的照片。

　　a. 附上　　　　　　b. 寄上　　　　　　c. 送上

6. 你要抓住 ＿＿＿ 机会医好他。

　　a. 一样　　　　　　b. 一般　　　　　　c. 一切

7. 吸烟是一种坏 ＿＿＿。

　　a. 爱好　　　　　　b. 习惯　　　　　　c. 常事

8. 好久没有收到你的信了，爸爸很 ＿＿＿ 你。

　　a. 挂念　　　　　　b. 挂着　　　　　　c. 着想

选词填空

用"到、规定、怎么、问、就是、别人、一点儿、后来、时候、吹"填空

我刚到上海的 ____，因为不懂上海话出了不少笑话。我 ____ 理发馆去刮脸洗头，理发员 ____ 我修面吗？我问他别人都修吗？他说 ____ 都修。我说："好吧，那我也修吧。"理发员就为我刮了脸。____ 他又问我："打头吗？"我想他 ____ 要打我？我就问他："你只打我一个人，还是来这里的顾客都打呀？"他说通通都打。我想，通通都打是这里的 ____，那我也打吧！理发员给我洗了头，____ 了风，完了拿过镜子一照说："好了！"我说："好啦？你怎么不打我了？""已经打过了。"理发员说。"打过了？怎么 ____ 不疼啊？"原来，在上海话里，修面就是刮脸，打头 ____ 洗头。

认字识词　Words with Known Characters

1. 查找出下列词汇的词义，并翻译成英文

退休	反对
误会	反义词
错误	同义词
靠近	同音词
到达	老伴儿

2. 翻译下列词汇，并找出其结构规律

干洗	慢跑
高考	大选
巧遇	冷烫
单打	双打
早婚	晚婚
紧靠	白吃

3. 请至少再找出5个同样结构的词

翻译练习　　　Translation

1. I saw a picture of Lao Wang's grandfather with a gown and pigtail yesterday at Lao Wang's house.

2. There are no buses on the road this morning, do you know what is happening?

3. I couldn't quite understand the accent (口音) of the people there at the beginning, but I have now got used to it.

4. What did you say? Surely he did not drive on the left this morning on his way to work?

5. This is a diversified world. In some countries, a man can have as many wives as he likes.

6. I lived in South Africa for five years and made a lot of friends there.

成语故事　　　The Stories Behind Chinese Idioms

狐假虎威

一天老虎 (tiger) 觉得肚子饿了，就到外面去找吃的东西。当他走到一片森林 (forest) 时，看到前面有只狐狸 (fox)。他觉得这正是个好机会，就扑 (jump) 过去把狐狸抓住了。

狐狸看见自己跑不掉了，就对老虎说："你怎么敢吃我？我是动物之王！"老虎当然不相信。狐狸马上接着说："你要是不信，就跟在我后面去森林里走一走，看看动物见了我是不是都会逃走。"老虎觉得它说得对。于是，它们一起向森林深处走去。狐狸在前面走，老虎在后面跟着，果然 (as expected)，森林里大大小小的动物看见老虎非常害怕，马上都跑掉了。老虎不知道这些动物是怕自己，以为他们是怕狐狸，所以就把狐狸放了。

实用练习　　**Module Practice**

从下列两个题目中任意选择一个题目作答

1. 给你的家人写一封信，字数为250到300个汉字。问候他们、告诉他们你的学习或工作情况，请他们不要挂念你。

2. 给一个男生/女生写一封信。告诉他/她你喜欢他/她，或者你爱他/她，你要做他/她的女/男朋友。

第三十八课　申请工作

Learning Objectives

Writing a covering letter

Writing your curriculum vitae

Learning about the doer + verb construction

生词 1　　　New Words

招聘	zhāopìn	动	recruit	招 attract	聘 invite to engage	
实习	shíxí	动	do intern work; work experience	实 actual, real		
实习生	shíxíshēng	名	intern			
有意者	yǒuyìzhě		person who is interested	意 desire	者 person	
工资	gōngzī	名	salary	资 capital		
求职信	qiúzhí xìn	名	job application letter			
居然	jūrán	副	unexpectedly			
牛皮大王	niúpí dàwáng	名	(colloquial) braggart, bullshitter			
才华	cáihuá	名	talent	才 talent	华 glamour	
出众	chūzhòng	形	outstanding	众 mass		
精通	jīngtōng	动/形	be proficient in	精 perfect		
夸张	kuāzhāng	动	exaggerate	夸 boast		
推销	tuīxiāo	动	sell, promote	推 push	销 sale	
老王卖瓜，自卖自夸			boast of one's own products			
以…（能力）		介	with… ability	能力 capability		

对话　　　　　　Dialogue

爱华：小王，你不是要找个公司实习吗？你看看这个广告。

小王：招聘实习生，每周工作六小时。有意者请寄简历来。

爱华：工资很高，每小时五十块。

小王：我马上跟他们联系。

爱华：你需要一封求职信和一份中文简历。

小王：我这儿有一份中文简历，你帮我看看，好不好？

爱华：好。……小王，没想到你居然是个牛皮大王！

小王：你说什么？！我哪儿吹了？

爱华："才华出众，精通汉语等五国语言"。

小王：这不是吹牛，只是有点儿夸张。

爱华：不是有点儿，而是太夸张了。

小王：不夸张怎么能把自己推销出去？

爱华：中国人最不喜欢这样的人，老王卖瓜，自卖自夸。

小王：我是姓王，可是我没有卖瓜。

爱华：好，你没有卖瓜。你不是精通汉语吗？怎么连这句话也不懂。学语言不学习文化是不行的。

小王：好，是我错了，我不该吹牛。你帮我改改，好不好？

爱华：你不怕推销不出去吗？

小王：不怕。以你的能力、我的资历，推销不出去才怪呢。

爱华：啊！你还在吹啊！

生词 2　　　　　New Words

毕业	bìyè	动	graduate	毕 complete
皇家	huángjiā	名	royal family	皇 emperor
苏格兰	Sūgélán	专名	Scotland	苏 revive; a surname　兰 orchid
目前	mùqián	副	at present	
熟悉	shúxi	动/形	be familiar with	悉 know
热情	rèqíng	形/名	enthusiastic; zeal	
胜任	shèngrèn	动	capable of, up to the job	胜 victory　任 take a post
国籍	guójí	名	nationality	籍 birthplace
传真	chuánzhēn	名	fax	传 pass
信箱	xìnxiāng	名	letter box	
学历	xuélì	名	education (history)	
至今	zhìjīn	副	up to present	至 to
海德	Hǎidé	专名	Hyde (transliteration)	
经历	jīnglì	名/动	experience	
建筑	jiànzhù	名/动	architecture, construction	建 build　筑 construct
分行	fēnháng	名	branch	
风险	fēngxiǎn	名	risk	
管理	guǎnlǐ	名/动	management	
技能	jìnéng	名	skill	技 skill
爱好	àihào	名	hobby	
爬山	pá shān	动	mountain climbing	
骑马	qí mǎ	动	horse riding	
卡拉OK	kālā-OK	名	karaoke	

课文 1　　　　Text One

求职信

尊敬的周小姐:

　　从报上我看到贵行正在招聘实习生,我对此工作十分感兴趣。特写此信申请。

　　我一直对银行业十分感兴趣。高中毕业后我就到皇家苏格兰银行实习了一年。我现在是伦敦欧洲商学院大二的学生,目前在北京语言大学学习汉语。我会说多种语言,熟悉银行业务,特别是信用卡业务。我为人热情、乐于助人。我想我一定能胜任这个工作。

　　附上我的简历。请查收。

　　此致

敬礼

求职人: 王京
2006年5月16日

课文 2　　　　　**Text Two**

个人简历

姓名：王京

出生年月：1982年2月7日

国籍：英国

联系地址：北京东城区建国路123号

联系方式：手机电话：013987556398　　　传真：010 32986745

电子信箱：daweiwang@yahoo.com.cn

学历：

2001年9月～至今　　　　　伦敦欧洲商学院学生

1994年9月～2000年7月　　　苏格兰金山中学学生

1988年8月～1994年7月　　　伦敦海德小学学生

工作经历：

2003年9月～至今　　　　　英语家庭教师

2000年8月～2001年8月　　　皇家苏格兰银行实习生

1998年7月～1998年9月　　　金山建筑公司实习生

工作兴趣：银行风险管理、信用卡业务、私人银行业务

技能：精通计算机；

　　　会说四国语言——英语、德语、意大利语、汉语

爱好：爬山、骑马、跳舞、卡拉OK、上网

语法注释　　Grammar Notes

1. **居然** -- an adverbial phrase indicating something unexpected or surprising. For example:

   ⑴ **居然会在这儿见到老同学！**

   What a surprise to meet an old classmate in here!

   ⑵ **他居然不打招呼就自己走了。**

   How could he leave on his own without telling anyone.

2. **推销不出去才怪呢。** -- "It would be strange if …" **呢** is necessary to indicate the view of the speaker. For example:

   ⑴ **她喜欢睡懒觉，这么早，她能起来才怪呢。**

   She likes to lie in; it would be strange if she were up so early.

   ⑵ **如果他再酒后开车，不出事才怪呢。**

   If he keeps on drinking and driving, it'll be surprising if he doesn't have an accident.

3. **为人热情、乐于助人** -- There are many four character phrases in Chinese, some from proverbs with stories behind them, some idiomatic phrases deriving from a long period of usage. You needs to pay close attention to such expressions as they are very typical of the language, and reflect the dichotomous and rhythmic aspects of the Chinese language.

中国人的谦虚

Traditionally, modesty is considered a virtue that a well-educated person should develop and possess. Chinese modesty is usually reflected in two ways: one should understate ones own achievements when talking about oneself (but it doesn't do much harm to overstate those of others); and one tends to deflect others' compliments by using what could be seen as a complete denial of the compliment (such as **不好，哪里哪里**). This can often lead to misunderstanding if you are not fully aware of this in Chinese culture. It is such that some Westerners even think that there is little difference between Chinese modesty and lies, and others find it tiring. But for Chinese, this is part of the culture of **礼让**. You only need to observe Chinese taking up their seats before a banquet to discover how this Chinese modesty reflects itself in the lives of Chinese people.

口语练习 　　Speaking Practice

小组活动

A: 你是一名求职者，正在接受公司的面试。别忘了，除了回答问题以外，你也应该问些问题，比如工资、住房、公司班车等等。

B: 你是公司的总经理，你正在面试求职者。你要问很多问题，比如工作经历、专业能力等等。

其他人：你们都是公司的高层领导，都正在参加面试新员工。你们每人至少要提问一个问题。

听力练习 　　Listening Practice

1.　a.不到一年　　　　　b.一年　　　　　　c.一年多

2.　a.他爸爸让他去　　　b.他没有钱了　　　c.他要练习汉语

3.　a.朋友很忙　　　　　b.朋友和他说英语　c.他没有中国朋友

4.　a.他的汉语不好　　　b.他的英语不好　　c.他的简历不够好

5.　a.十几个人　　　　　b.几十个人　　　　c.几百个人

6.　a.十几个人　　　　　b.几十个人　　　　c.几百个人

7.　a.工作少　　　　　　b.学历不够高　　　c.高不成低不就

8.　a.求职信　　　　　　b.简历　　　　　　c.名片

语法练习 　　Grammar Practice

单项选择

1.　伦敦大学正在 ＿＿＿＿ 数学讲师，你可以去试试。

　　a.招聘　　　　　b.录取　　　　　c.口试

2.　他本来是个人见人爱的好学生，没想到他 ＿＿＿＿ 做出这种事情来。

　　a.居然　　　　　b.突然　　　　　c.虽然

3.　他的女朋友 ＿＿＿＿ 电脑，你可以叫她看一看你的电脑有什么毛病。

　　a.普通　　　　　b.精通　　　　　c.打通

4.　他们带了样品，去美国 ＿＿＿＿ 他们的产品。

　　a.推行　　　　　b.推销　　　　　c.推卖

5. 所有的外国留学生，毕业以后都可以在英国 ____ 一年。

    a. 练习   b. 实习   c. 学习

6. 就是你把你自己 ____ 上天，人们还是不相信你的。

    a. 说   b. 告诉   c. 吹

7. 这个工作很重要，你看他能不能 ____？

    a. 担任   b. 胜任   c. 当

8. 通知发出去已经一个星期了，可是 ____ 还没有人报名。

    a. 今天   b. 今后   c. 至今

选词填空

用"广告、招聘、精通、马上、居然、熟练、种、使用、看着、没想到"填空

      一个公司要 ____ 一名新职员，于是就在报纸上登出一份广告说："招聘文职人员，要会打字、懂电脑、____ 两种语言。符合条件者机会平等。"____ 第二天，第一个来应聘的 ____ 是一条狗。"对不起，我不能招聘一条狗。"经理说。狗不服气，拿出了 ____ 和他讲理。经理没有办法，只好问道："你会打字吗？"那条狗 ____ 走到打字机前打了一封信。"你懂得怎样 ____ 电脑吗？"经理又问。那条狗又坐在一台电脑前，非常 ____ 地用起电脑来。经理有点儿急了，"我需要的雇员要会说两 ____ 语言，你会吗？" 那条狗得意地 ____ 经理说："汪！喵！"

> 认字识词　　**Words with Known Characters**

1. 查找出下列词汇的词义，并翻译成英文

    西瓜   建造

    兰花   大众

    事实   高科技

    传球   资本

    皇上   胜利

2. 翻译下列词汇 ，并找出其结构规律

中国造	心算
口吃	自助
自主	师传
手写	友爱
云游	日出
笔录	鱼死网破

3. 请至少再找出5个同样结构的词

翻译练习　　　**Translation**

1. I didn't expect him to be so fond of boasting.

2. I have heard that your company is recruiting interns, I am very interested in this (job).

3. Our teacher is very talented. she draws very well.

4. Last year I went to quite a few places in China. Chinese people are all very warm.

5. What are your hobbies? I like climbing, riding, dancing and reading.

6. I have a lot of experience in banking, and I believe that I am capable of doing the job.

成语故事　　　**The Stories Behind Chinese Idioms**

买椟(dú)还珠

从前有一个楚国人，他有一颗(kē) (a measure word) 漂亮的珍珠(zhēnzhū) (pearl)。他打算把这颗珍珠卖出去。为了卖个好价钱，他请人做了一个精致(jīngzhì) (elegant) 的盒子（即椟）。然后，他将珍珠小心地放进盒子里，拿到市场上去卖。

到市场上不久，有一个人看到了这个盒子，他非常喜欢，出高价将盒子买了下来。可是没走几步他又回来了。楚人以为他后悔(huǐ) (regret) 了要退货 (return goods)，可是他走到楚人跟前，将盒子打开，取出里面的珍珠交给楚人说："先生，您的珍珠忘在盒子里了。"他将珍珠交给了楚人，然后拿着空木盒子走了。

实用练习 **Module Practice**

1. 写一份你自己的简历

    注意：这份简历一定要真实，你可以寄给相关公司求职。

2. 写一封求职信

    你最想干什么工作，你就写信求什么职，什么工作都可以。

第三十九课　购物

Learning Objectives

Talking about shopping and where to shop

Understanding bargaining tips and practice

Learning about the verb + complement construction

生词 1　　　　　New Words

陪	péi	动	accompany		
购物	gòu wù	动/名	(go) shopping	购	purchase
逛	guàng	动	walk round (shops), ramble, stroll		
随便	suíbiàn	副	casually; as you like	随	follow
牙膏	yágāo	名	toothpaste	膏	paste
牙刷	yáshuā	名	tooth brush	刷	brush
香皂	xiāngzào	名	toilet soap	皂	soap
肥皂	féizào	名	soap	肥	fat
齐	qí	形	full, complete		
齐全	qíquán	形	complete		
必要	bìyào	名/形	necessity; necessary		
百货大楼	bǎihuò dàlóu	名	department store		
不得了	bùdéliǎo	副	(colloquial) very much		
自由市场	zìyóu shìchǎng	名	free market	由	reason; to
物美价廉	wùměi-jiàlián	形	(product) cheap but good	廉	cheap
与其…不如	yǔqí…bùrú	连	rather…than…	与 with 其 that

对话 1　　　**Dialogue One**

王京：谢谢你陪我上街购物。

爱华：不用谢，我最喜欢逛商店了。

王京：那我们今天就好好逛逛。

爱华：你都打算买什么？

王京：随便逛逛，看到什么好就买什么。

爱华：牙膏、牙刷、香皂、肥皂你都买齐了吗？

王京：与其说是买齐了，不如说是带齐了。这些东西我都是从英国带来的。

爱华：天啊，有这个必要吗？！

王京：我用惯了西方的牌子，怕在中国买不到。

爱华：我带你去百货大楼看看，那里的西方日用品多得不得了。

王京：那可太好了！走，我们去百货大楼。

爱华：北京的自由市场也不错。

王京：那里的东西多吗？

爱华：多！那里要什么有什么，而且物美价廉。

王京：那我们还等什么，去自由市场！

生词 2   New Words

小伙子	xiǎohuǒzi	名	young lad	
牛仔裤	niúzǎikù	名	jeans	仔 cub, child
洞	dòng	名	hole	
故意	gùyì	副	intentionally	故 intentionally; cause; old
款式	kuǎnshì	名	style, fashion	
骗	piàn	动	cheat, deceive	
装	zhuāng	动	put, hold	
狗熊	gǒuxióng	名	black bear, a coward	
毛裤	máokù	名	long woollen underpants	
单裤	dānkù	名	unlined trousers, single layer of outer trousers	
过冬	guò dōng	动	spend winter, go through winter	
暖气	nuǎnqì	名	central heating	
姑娘	gūniang	名	girl	姑 auntie, woman 娘 mother
长裙	chángqún	名	long skirt	
超短裙	chāoduǎnqún	名	mini skirt	
追	zhuī	动	court, chase, pursue	
连衣裙	liányīqún	名	long dress	
优惠价	yōuhuìjià	名	preferential, special price 优 excellent 惠 benefit	
打折	dǎ zhé	动	give discount 折 discount, fold, break	
大娘	dàniáng	名	aunty, granny	
走神	zǒu shén	动	be distracted or absent minded, not concentrating	
或者	huòzhě	连	or	
连忙	liánmáng	副	hurriedly	
当场	dāngchǎng	副	on the spot, there and then	
死去活来	sǐqù-huólái	形	hovering between life and death, very much	
骂	mà	动	swear at, curse	
千万	qiānwàn	副	absolutely, definitely, be sure to, must 万 ten thousand	

补充词汇   Additional Vocabulary

专卖店	zhuānmàidiàn	specialist store	帽子	màozi	hat, cap
礼品店	lǐpǐndiàn	gift shop	手套	shǒutào	gloves
精品店	jīngpǐndiàn	boutique	围巾	wéijīn	scarf, muffler
眼镜店	yǎnjìngdiàn	optician's	风衣	fēngyī	overcoat
晚礼服	wǎnlǐfú	evening wear	皮靴	píxuē	leather boots
休闲装	xiūxiánzhuāng	casual dress	高跟鞋	gāogēnxié	high heel shoes

对话 2　　Dialogue Two

大娘：小伙子，你需要买一条新牛仔裤了。

小王：大娘，你搞错了，我裤子上的洞是故意弄破的。

大娘：我知道，可是这已经不是最新款式了。

小王：不会吧，我来之前刚买的。

大娘：我不会骗你的，你看，这才是现在流行的款式。

小于：这款式不错，肥肥大大的，里面能装一头狗熊。

大娘：天气冷了，里面加条毛裤正好。

小王：我只穿单裤，从来没穿过毛裤。

大娘：看来你还没在北京过过冬，北京这儿冬天冷得很。

小于：有暖气，没关系。

大娘：姑娘，你也买条长裙吧，你那超短裙过不了冬。

小于：大娘，长裙太贵了，我买不起。

大娘：瞧你说的，你有个外国男朋友，怎么会买不起？！

小王：大娘，她还不是我的女朋友。

大娘：那就快追！来，这条连衣裙昨天刚到，她穿正好。

小王：真漂亮！我们要了。

小于：不行不行，价格太贵了！给个优惠价吧？

大娘：好，我打八折卖给你们，谁叫我一见到你们就喜欢呢！

小王：谢谢大娘。

"东西" 这东西真是个怪 "东西"

学习 "东西" 那一课时，我走神了。后来老师问我知道不知道怎么用 "东西" 一词。我说："当然知道。我们可以说桌子是 '东西'，可是不能说 '你是东西' 或者 '我是东西'，因为我们都不是 '东西'。" 老师一听急了，忙说："不对，不对，不能说 '我不是东西'。" 我连忙说："啊，对不起，你是东西。" 老师说："也不能说 '你是东西'。" 我一听也急了 "那你到底是什么东西？" 老师当场气得半死，同学们乐得死去活来。

现在我知道了 "你不是东西" 是骂人的话，"你是什么东西" 也是骂人的话。"东西" 这东西真是个怪 "东西"，使用 "东西" 这个词时可得千万小心哪。

北方人冬天的着装

Generally speaking, winter is cold and windy in northern China. Temperatures can be as cold as minus 20 degrees centigrade, so people do need to wrap up warm, which is why 毛裤 or even 棉裤 (cotton padded trousers) are common winter clothing. Padded jackets are most common, especially those padded with feathers (羽绒服), which have virtually replaced the traditional cotton padded ones (棉袄). Today newer fibres are used for underwear, often called 中空棉 or 保暖服. However, with the influence of the West, it is becoming increasingly common for some women of younger generation to brave the cold winter just wearing a skirt. Chinese often joke about this as having 风度 (fashionable style) at the expense of 温度 (temperature).

语法注释　　Grammar Notes

1. **那我们还等什么？** -- "Then what are we waiting for?"

2. **大娘** -- Honorifics such as this are common in Chinese, but vary from place to place in terms of to whom and when to use. This term is similar to **大妈** and tends to be used to address women older than your own parents.

3. **我不会骗你的**。 -- "I am not trying to cheat you." This is a **是**...**的** construction with the **是** omitted.

4. **我打八折卖给你们**。 -- **打八折** is a 20% discount, **七折** 30% off; 50% can be expressed as **打五折** or **打对折**.

5. **谁叫我一见到你们就喜欢呢？** -- "I couldn't help liking you at first sight." It is framed as a rhetorical question ("Who made me like you at first sight?"), and is often used to express the idea that it is someone's own responsibility for what happens. **呢** is often used at the end. For example:
   (1) **谁叫你不去呢？那儿好玩极了**。
   Why didn't you go? It was great there.
   (2) **谁叫他不仔细一点呢？他应该考上的**。
   Why wasn't he a bit more careful? He should have passed.

6. **或者** -- means "or" in a statement, while **还是** is used in a question. For example:
   (1) **明天或者你来、或者我去，怎么都行**。
   Tomorrow either you come here or I'll go there, either way is fine.
   (2) **您要买长裙还是短裙？**
   Do you want to buy a long skirt or a short one?

口语练习   Speaking Practice

角色扮演

1. A: 你是顾客，要在大商场里买一件合身的衣服。

   B: 你是售货员，你要设法卖件衣服给他/她。

2. A: 你是顾客，要在自由市场讨价还价，买一件你喜欢的商品。

   B: 你是买东西的店主，你要设法多卖几块钱。

听力练习   Listening Practice

1. a. 三千   b. 二千   c. 一千
2. a. 有工作   b. 有女朋友   c. 女朋友
3. a. 女朋友的爸妈   b. 他爸妈   c. 女朋友请他去她家过年
4. a. 太贵了   b. 钱包不见了   c. 没有合适的
5. a. 昨天   b. 刚才   c. 出门的时候
6. a. 他像个小偷   b. 他跟随他们   c. 他在跑
7. a. 他不是小偷   b. 他跑掉了   c. 他是警察的朋友
8. a. 他抓住了小偷   b. 他报告了警察   c. 他告诉了王力

语法练习   Grammar Practice

单项选择

1. 你爸爸妈妈来看你，你应该 ____ 他们好好玩几天。

   a. 陪   b. 跟   c. 同

2. 我们现在 ____ 吃点儿点心，等会儿一起到饭店里去吃饭。

   a. 顺便   b. 方便   c. 随便

3. 你为什么 ____ 跟我过不去呢？

   a. 故意   b. 好意   c. 乐意

4. 这几天我忙得 ____。

   a. 不得了   b. 了不得   c. 了不起

5. 你问问他有没有 _____ 这样做。

    a. 必得   b. 必要   c. 必然

6. 我见他进来，_____ 站起来打招呼。

    a. 连接   b. 连连   c. 连忙

7. 路上车子很多，你得多加 _____。

    a. 小心   b. 留心   c. 信心

8. 你不要 _____ 我，这件事的真相我早都知道了。

    a. 听   b. 骗   c. 信

选词填空

用"没有、一、与其、来、不必、往年、也、过、还是、快"填空

    圣诞节 _____ 到了，这是我在中国过的第一个圣诞节，_____ 是我第一次离开老家伦敦，离开亲人，在外面一个人 _____ 圣诞节。我很想念远在英国的亲人。_____ 这个时候，人们都在忙着准备过节的礼物。_____ 到周末，牛津街到处都是人。大公司，小商店，_____ 一家不是人山人海的。虽然北京这里也开始了圣诞销售，可是比起伦敦 _____，这里冷清多了，因为中国人不过圣诞节。我在这里没有很多朋友，所以今年 _____ 准备很多礼物，要买的也早已买好了。可是周末我 _____ 想到王府井大街去逛逛。_____ 说是去买东西，倒不如说是去找找感觉。

认字识词   Words with Known Characters

1. 查找出下列词汇的词义，并翻译成英文

       故事   陪同

       理由   骗子

       鞋刷   姑姑

       随和   购买

       随身听   药膏

2. 翻译下列词汇，并找出其结构规律

改变	说明
放大	完成
识破	拉平
表明	推进
刷新	说开
登高	跌倒

3. 请至少再找出5个同样结构的词

翻译练习　　Translation

1. After being cheated by him a few times, we no longer believe what he says.

2. In January many shops in the UK sell their goods at a discount.

3. My parents like to go shopping at free markets as the things there are good and cheap.

4. We must meet up next week. Should I go to your place or will you come to mine?

5. She intentionally bought this big size dress as she was told it would be the fashion this summer.

6. She is the most beautiful girl in our school and there are lots of boys chasing her.

成语故事　　The Stories Behind Chinese Idioms

_{wàngméizhǐkě}
望梅止渴

有一年夏天，曹操 _{cáocāo}（a famous leader in the Three Kingdoms period）带兵 _{bīng}（soldiers）去打仗。这天天气特别热，到了中午，大家都渴得不得了，所以走得越来越慢了。

曹操心里很是着急。可是到哪儿去找水呢？他把向导（guide）找来，小声（in a low voice）地问他："这附近有没有水？"向导说："泉水（spring）在山的那一边，要过去得走好几个小时。"曹操想了一下说，"不行，时间来不及。"他看了看前边的树林 _{shùlín}（woods），回头对向导说："你什么也别说，我来想办法。"他骑马跑到队伍前面，大声对士兵 _{shìbīng}（soldiers）说："士兵们，我知道前面有一大片<u>梅林</u>（plum grove），那里的梅子又大又好吃，我们快点赶路，过了这个山就到梅林了！"士兵们一听，都好像已经吃到了梅子，<u>口水</u>（saliva）都流了出来，<u>脚步</u>（foot steps）也就加快了许多。

实用练习　　Module Practice

1. 你想让你的朋友帮你买一样东西。你给他／她写一张纸条，说明你要的东西的大小、款式、价格、颜色等等。

2. 写一篇短文，介绍一件商品。字数在200字左右。

第四十课 故宫

Learning Objectives

Talking about sightseeing and trips

Learning the written style and the use of 所 plus verb

Learning about the acronyms.

生词 1　　　　New Words

同志	tóngzhì	名	comrade		
故宫	Gùgōng	名	Imperial Palace	故 old	宫 palace
博物馆	bówùguǎn	名	museum	博 vast, extensive	
参观	cānguān	动	visit and tour around (a place)	观 look, observe	
天安门	Tiān'ānmén	专名	Tian'anmen	安 peace	
城楼	chénglóu	名	gate tower, rostrum		
通票	tōngpiào	名	multiple-venue ticket		
人民大会堂	Rénmín Dàhuìtáng	专名	The Great Hall of the People		
停止	tíngzhǐ	动	stop	止 stop	
外宾	wàibīn	名	foreign guest	宾 guest	
来访	láifǎng	动	come on a visit	访 visit	
总理	zǒnglǐ	名	premier, prime minister		
举行	jǔxíng	动	hold, take place	举 hold up	
宴会	yànhuì	名	banquet	宴 formal meal, banquet	
毛主席	Máo Zhǔxí	专名	Chairman Mao	主 main	席 seat
纪念堂	jìniàntáng	名	memorial hall	堂 hall	
仪式	yíshì	名	rite, ceremony	仪 ceremony, appearance	
结束	jiéshù	动	finish, end	束 tie, control	

对话 1　　Dialogue One

王小明：同志，我买一张故宫博物馆的门票。

售票员：60块一张。

王小明：听说学生优惠，这是我的学生证。

售票员：对，学生20块一张。

王小明：我还想参观天安门和人民大会堂，你们卖不卖通票？

售票员：对不起，我们现在还没有这个业务。

王小明：人民大会堂今天好像停止参观，你知道为什么吗？

售票员：今天有重要外宾来访，总理要在那儿举行欢迎宴会。

王小明：那我还可以参观毛主席纪念堂吗？

售票员：可以，不过得等到欢迎仪式结束之后。

王小明：我先参观故宫，一个小时后出来正好。

售票员：故宫很大，没有两三个小时你出不来。

王小明：是吗？那我得赶快进去。谢谢。

售票员：不客气。

生词 2　　　　New Words

任何	rènhé	名	any	何	which
禁止	jìnzhǐ	动	forbid	禁	forbid
景点	jǐngdiǎn	名	places of interest	景	scene
格外	géwài	副	especially, exceptionally		
皇宫	huánggōng	名	royal palace		
皇帝	huángdì	名	emperor	帝	emperor, imperial
紫禁城	Zǐjìnchéng	专名	Forbidden City		
称为	chēngwéi	动	be called as	称	call; say
占地	zhàndì	动	occupy an area of	占	occupy
平方米	píngfāngmǐ	名	square metre	米	meter, rice
现存	xiàncún	形	currently existing, surviving		
规模	guīmó	名	scale	模	pattern
保存	bǎocún	动	preserve		
古代	gǔdài	名	ancient times	古	ancient
古建筑群	gǔ jiànzhùqún	名	cluster of ancient buildings	群	cluster, group
天文学	tiānwénxué	名	astronomy		
紫微星	zǐwēixīng	专名	North Star	微	small, tiny
中天	zhōngtiān	名	centre of cosmos		
所在	suǒzài	名	place; place where something exists		
所	suǒ	助	which that		
天帝	tiāndì	名	celestial emperor (Emperor of the Heaven)		
因而	yīnér	连	thus, therefore		
真龙天子	zhēnlóng tiānzǐ	名	real son of the dragon (emperor)		
禁地	jìndì	名	forbidden place		
出入	chūrù	动	go in and out; entry and exit		

补充词汇　　Additional Vocabulary

颐和园	Yíhéyuán	Summer Palace	禁止照相	jìnzhǐ zhàoxiàng	No Photograph
北海公园	Běihǎi Gōngyuán	Beihai Park	禁止吸烟	jìnzhǐ xīyān	No Smoking
天坛公园	Tiántán Gōngyuán	Temple of Heaven	禁止钓鱼	jìnzhǐ diàoyú	No Fishing
自然博物馆	Zìrán Bówùguǎn	Natural Museum	请勿喧哗	qǐng wù xuānhuá	Be quiet
历史博物馆	Lìshǐ Bówùguǎn	History Museum	请勿入内	qǐng wù rù nèi	No Entry
首都博物馆	Shǒudū Bówùguǎn	Capital Museum	闲人免进	xiánrén miǎnjìn	Staff Only

对话 2　　　Dialogue Two

小王：请问，参观毛主席纪念堂是在这儿排队吗？

小李：是的，不过你得先去存包。

小王：我的包里没什么东西。

小李：参观纪念堂不准带任何东西。

小王：照相机也不能带吗？

小李：不能。里面禁止照相。

小王：请问存包处在哪儿？

小李：在东面儿。你看，好多人在那儿排队。

小王：这么长的队！我不应该今天来。

小李：天天都是这样。

小王：中国人真多。

小李：北京是重要的旅游景点，人格外多。

课文　　　　　　Text

故宫

故宫博物馆位于北京市中心，是明、清两代的皇宫，先后居住过24位皇帝。明清时称为紫禁城，1925年开始称为故宫。故宫博物馆占地七十二万多平方米，有房屋九千多间，是当今世界上现存规模最大、保存最完好的古代皇宫建筑群。

这座故宫为什么称为紫禁城呢？原来，中国古代天文学认为紫微星居于中天，是天帝所在。因而，把天帝所居住的天宫叫做紫宫。皇帝自称是天帝的儿子，是真龙天子，因而他们所居住的皇宫也被称为紫宫。皇宫是禁地，是不能随便出入的，所以又被称为紫禁城。

参观中国的名胜古迹

Most places of historical interest in China need entry tickets (门票). Many such places are actually quite extensive, such as the Ming Tombs (十三陵) in Beijing, which consists of about a dozen of different exhibitions, and Zhou Zhuang (周庄) in Shanghai, which is a small village with a number of different museums. It is common in China that in the same place of interest visitors need to buy separate entry tickets for different exhibitions or shows. But more and more places of this kind offer multi-venue tickets (联票). Like anywhere else, it is usually cheaper to get the multi-venue entry ticket.

语法注释   **Grammar Notes**

1. **没有两三个小时你出不来**。 -- "You won't get round in less than two or three hours."
    Note the use of double negation here.

2. **参观纪念堂不准带任何东西**。 -- Note the use of an interrogative with negation indicating inclusiveness; this is the same with the interrogative pronouns **谁、什么** etc. For example:

    (1) **他现在心情不好，任何人都不想见**。

    He is not very happy at the moment, and does not want to see anyone at all.

    (2) **她经常骗人，所以她现在说任何话，大家都不信了**。

    She's always deceiving people so nobody believes a word she says now.

3. **天帝所居住的天宫** -- Used as a particle, **所** plus a verb creates a more formal written style but without adding any additional meaning to the new construction, (thus it can be omitted). For example:

    (1) **天帝所居住的天宫 = 天帝居住的天宫**

    Heavenly Palace inhabited by the Celestial Emperor.

    (2) **她所说的话、所做的事 = 她说的话、做的事**

    What she says, what she does.

4. **参观与访问的区别** -- **参观** and **访问** are both translated as "visit" in English, but you can see the difference through the Chinese characters. **参观** is mainly visual "see", while **访问** is more oral "see" and "ask". So you can **参观** or **访问** an institution，but you can only **参观** a place and **访问** a friend. For example:

    (1) **欢迎你们参观/访问我们公司**。

    You are welcome to visit our company.

    (2) **欢迎参观我们的校园**。

    You are welcome to visit our campus.

    (3) **我明天要去访问一名老作家**。

    I am going to pay a visit to an old writer tomorrow.

口语练习　　Speaking Practice

小组活动

　　每人介绍一个你去过、或者听说过的中国有意思的地方。如果你什么地方都没去过也没有听说过，上网查找一个。如果你去过，请告诉大家有关门票等情况。

听力练习　　Listening Practice

1. a.骑马　　　　　b.爬山　　　　　c.打篮球
2. a.读书　　　　　b.参加球赛　　　c.旅游
3. a.北海公园　　　b.故宫　　　　　c.长城
4. a.爬长城　　　　b.看儿子　　　　c.参观故宫
5. a.王京会花钱了　b.王京不计较钱了　c.王京会导游了
6. a.帮助别人　　　b.要小费　　　　c.白用别人
7. a.香港　　　　　b.上海　　　　　c.西安
8. a.同学　　　　　b.他自己　　　　c.同学的妹妹

语法练习　　Grammar Practice

单项选择

1. 今天下午我们去 ____ 博物馆，好吗？
   a.访问　　　　　b.参观　　　　　c.观光
2. 我们这学期什么时候 ____？
   a.完成　　　　　b.结果　　　　　c.结束
3. 从今天开始，他们公司 ____ 营业。
   a.停止　　　　　b.停顿　　　　　c.停车
4. 2008年的奥运会将在中国北京 ____。
   a.进行　　　　　b.举行　　　　　c.举起
5. 这儿 ____ 机动车辆通行。
   a.停止　　　　　b.阻止　　　　　c.禁止

6. 这次运动会的 ＿＿＿＿ 很大。

    a. 规模   b. 规定   c. 规格

7. 这儿经常有车辆 ＿＿＿＿，请你不要在这儿放东西。

    a. 里外   b. 上下   c. 出入

8. 从明年开始，＿＿＿＿ 人都不准在公共场合吸烟。

    a. 任何   b. 大多数   c. 不少

选词填空

用"住下、离开、所在、名称、真的、尽管、仔细地、写着、因此、才"填空

    有一个老外到中国去旅游。当天晚上 ＿＿＿＿ 以后，他想一个人出去逛逛这个城市。他不懂汉语，＿＿＿＿ 怕迷路回不了旅馆。于是，他在 ＿＿＿＿ 旅馆的第一个路口停下来，拿出笔记本，＿＿＿＿ 记下了那家旅馆所在街道的街名，然后放心地走了。后来他 ＿＿＿＿ 迷路了，他在街上转了好几小时 ＿＿＿＿ 找到一个警察所。由于语言不通，警察搞不明白他的意思。于是他把记着街道 ＿＿＿＿ 的笔记本给警察看，可是警察还是不明白。后来警察请来了一位翻译，这位老外对翻译说："＿＿＿＿ 我不知道旅馆的名称，但是我知道旅馆 ＿＿＿＿ 街道的名称。"说着，他把笔记本交给翻译。翻译一看，纸上 ＿＿＿＿：单行道。

> 认字识词   **Words with Known Characters**

1. 查找出下列词汇的词义，并翻译成英文

博士	帝国
教堂	模式
米色	如何
主人	主任
微观	入口

2. 写出下列词汇的完全形式

中行	港商
北师大	女友
高校	人大
交警	亚运会
影星	超女
名医	数理化

3. 请至少再找出5个同样结构的词

翻译练习　　　Translation

1. The doctor does not allow you to eat anything before your medical check up.

2. The premier is going to hold a welcome banquet for him in the Great Hall of the People today.

3. Things are very expensive in that country. You won't be able to go for a holiday without taking a few thousand US dollars.

4. This group of buildings occupies about 5000 square metres.

5. Do you know the name of the last emperor in China?

6. Though what he said was not entirely true, nevertheless I don't think he meant to cheat you.

成语故事　The Stories Behind Chinese Idioms

yúgōngyíshān
愚公移山

　　从前有一位老人，住在华北，名叫愚公。他的家门南面有两座大山挡住 (dǎngzhù)

(blocked) 了他家的出路。这两座山一座叫做太行山，一座叫做王屋山。愚公下

决心率领 (shuàilǐng) (lead) 他的儿子们把这两座大山搬走。有个名叫智叟 (zhìsǒu) 的老头子看了

发笑，说："你们这样干太愚蠢 (yúchǔn) (stupid) 了，你们父子数人要挖掉 (wādiào) (dig away) 这

样两座大山是完全不可能的。"愚公回答说："我死了以后有我的儿子，儿

子死了又有孙子，子子孙孙是不会穷尽 (jìn) (end) 的。这两座山虽然很高，却是不

会再增^{zēng}高 (grow) 了，挖一点就会少一点，有什么挖不平呢？"愚公每天挖山不止。这件事感动 (be moved) 了天帝，他就派了两个神仙^{shénxiān} (immortal) 下凡 (come down to the world)，把这两座山背走了。

实用练习　　Module Practice

写一篇文章，介绍一下北京，并将这篇文章通过电子邮件发送给你的朋友。文章越长越好，你要挑战自己，看看自己最长能写多长。

附录一 Appendix 1

组词练习 Word Game

How many Chinese words and phrases can you find in the following table? They are formed only with the neighbouring characters, but characters can be used more than once, and the formation can be in any direction, up down, left right, or vice verse, and diagonally too.

住	处	务	商	检	航	天	真	览	游
户	账	询	查	模	失	算	阅	街	逛
德	道	空	问	规	约	预	教	读	看
址	知	名	话	讲	定	购	堂	书	法
地	遍	通	说	理	假	型	证	念	想
区	普	常	经	管	发	准	备	思	纪
别	单	装	历	染	开	会	体	健	意
性	女	简	阴	阳	错	误	员	身	康
格	表	报	校	怪	惯	职	客	房	东
外	达	到	学	习	死	美	观	大	方
语	内	部	分	期	活	景	卡	参	款
调	音	乐	队	选	星	车	用	箱	存
动	录	俱	进	修	座	明	信	片	子
取	像	目	前	行	银	码	密	封	面

附录二 Appendix 2

听力原文 Listening Scripts

Warming Up Lesson
听力练习－Listening Practice

There is a paragraph in this section. Listen carefully and circle the correct answer to each question.

Dialogue 1

我昨天在出租车上把我的行李丢了。我拿了好多行李，很累，可是司机总是跟我说话，问这问那。下车的时候，我只拿了汽车后备箱里的两个大箱子，忘了拿座位上的小箱子。小箱子里面有我每天都要用的东西，还有我从英国给朋友带来的生日礼物。我很生气也很着急，可是不知道怎么办才好，昨天一晚上都没睡好觉。没想到今天早上八点钟就有人来找我，是楼下看门的师傅，他说有人来给我送东西。我一看，正是昨天的司机，他手里提着我的小箱子。原来司机发现了我的箱子，看到上面有我的行李卡，卡上有我的地址，就把箱子给我送来了。我当时要给他一百块钱，可是他就是不收，我就请他到一家大饭店吃了一顿西餐。明天等我有时间，我一定写封信给出租车公司的老板，谢谢这位好司机。

问题

1. "我"在哪里把（行李）小箱子丢了？

2. "我"为什么把小箱子丢了？

3. 小箱子里面有什么？

4. 发现小箱子丢了以后，"我"的心情怎么样？

5. 今天早上谁来找"我"？

6. 司机从哪儿看到"我"的地址？

7. "我"为什么要请司机吃饭？

8. "我"要给谁写信？

Lesson 31

听力练习- Listening Practice

There are two listening materials in this section. Listen carefully and circle the correct answer to each question. Each listening material contains four questions.

Dialogue 1

　　杰克(Jack)是英国苏格兰(Scotland)人，他是格拉斯哥(Glasgow)大学中文系的学生，他很喜欢中国文学。今年他到北京大学中文系学习，还没有开学，他就早早来到了北京。他游览了很多名胜古迹， 也参观了北京图书馆。他说他现在更喜欢中国文化了。

　　今天是北京大学开学的第一天。他高高兴兴地去北京大学注册报到，可是到了注册站，他找不到录取通知书了。他马上跑回宿舍，找遍了他的房间，还是找不到他的录取通知书。最后他想起来了，昨天他带了录取通知书去地铁站买月票，回来以后把通知书和月票都放在书包里了。可是书包在哪儿呢？啊，想起来了！书包让他的朋友王英拿走了！

　　问题

　　1. 杰克是哪国人？

　　2. 开学前他做什么了？

　　3. 开学的那天他在找什么？

　　4. 为什么没有找到？

Dialogue 2

老师：下一位！

杰克：您好。我，我……

老师：你的护照和录取通知书呢？

杰克：这是我的护照，可是我的录取通知书……

老师：丢了？

杰克：我放在包里，可是包被我的朋友拿走了。

老师：那你打电话让他送来。

杰克：他现在不在北京，所以……真对不起。您能不能帮帮我？

老师：你是哪个系的？学什么专业？

杰克：我是中文系的，我学中国现代文学。

老师：你是读学位的还是进修的？

杰克：我是读学位的。

老师：好，我查一下电脑……找到了。我给你系里打个电话，你等一会儿。

杰克：谢谢。

老师：行了！请你到那边去交费。

杰克：谢谢你了。再见。

老师：不谢，再见！

问题

5. 注册老师向杰克要录取通知书和什么？

6. 杰克要到哪个系学习？

7. 发现杰克没带录取通知书，注册老师做了什么？

8. 最后注册老师让杰克去哪儿了？

Lesson 32

听力练习- Listening Practice

There are two listening materials in this section. Listen carefully and circle the correct answer to each question. Each listening material contains five questions.

Dialogue 1

马里：小姐，你真漂亮，我能请你跳舞吗？

小云：谢谢，你很会说话。

马里：是吗？你叫什么名字？

小云：我叫张小云。你呢？

马里：我叫马里。你的舞跳得很好，你一定常常参加舞会吧？

小云：也不常常参加。我爸爸妈妈不让。

马里：你爸爸妈妈一定都是老师吧？

小云：对，他们都是教书的。

马里：他们教什么呢？

小云：我爸爸在北大教数学，我妈妈在音乐学院教音乐。

马里：真巧！我也是音乐学院的学生，今天才刚注册。你妈妈姓什么？

小云：我妈姓方，可是她这学期上不了班了。

马里：为什么？

小云：我妈妈开车出事了，上星期才刚刚出院。

马里：我能去看看她吗？

小云：当然可以。你什么时候来我家？

马里：明天晚上好吗？

小云：好。

问题

1. 小云和马里是在哪儿认识的？

2. 小云的爸爸妈妈是做什么工作的？

3. 马里学什么专业？

4. 小云的妈妈为什么这学期不教课？

5. 马里什么时候去看小云的妈妈？

Dialogue 2

中国人和美国人一样，都很喜欢打篮球。在中国，差不多每个大学、中学或小学都有篮球场地。下午下课以后，同学们都喜欢去打篮球。中国有一个年轻人篮球打得很好。他是上海人，他出生于1980年9月12日，身高2米26，体重125公斤。他妈妈以前也是个很有名的篮球运动员。这个人就是姚明。现在他在美国打球。你知道姚明的球衣是多少号吗？是西方人不喜欢的13号。

问题

6. 下午下课以后，中国学生喜欢做什么？

7. 中国最有名的篮球运动员叫什么名字？

8. 他妈妈以前做什么工作？

9. 他的身高是多少？

10.他的球衣是多少号？

Lesson 33

听力练习- Listening Practice

There are two listening materials in this section. Listen carefully and circle the correct answer to each question. Each listening material contains four questions.

Dialogue 1

　　杰克来到北京以后，就到北京王府井的中国银行开了一个账户。他把带来的旅行支票存进了银行的账户里，可是他还没有信用卡，也没有拿到提款卡。今天他想去取点儿钱，他来到了银行，银行里人很多。他只好站在那里等。这要等多长时间啊？他一边排队，一边看书。一个服务员走过来问他："先生，你也取款吗？"他说是的。那个服务员告诉他，他应该去另一边排队。他跟着那个服务员来到了另一个窗口，那里一个人也没有。原来这是专门给外汇账户开的窗口。

　　问题

　　1. 杰克在哪儿开的账户？

　　2. 他是怎么把外汇带进中国的？

　　3. 看到银行里人很多，杰克做了什么？

　　4. 为什么他能到另一个窗口取钱？

Dialogue 2

职员：您好，先生。

杰克：您好，我想取三千美元。

职员：请您下个星期来取。我们支行不保存美元，要到总行去取。所以你得提前一个星期通知我们。

杰克：那我不取美元了，我要人民币。我要兑换三百美元的人民币。

职员：那可以。请您填一张取款单，你带证件了吗？

杰克：带了，这是我的护照。

职员：好，请输入你的密码。

杰克：好。这样行了吗？

职员：您的密码不对。请您再试一下。

杰克：什么，怎么会不对呢？我再试试。

职员：还是不对。

杰克：我能再试一下吗？

职员：可以。对不起，您的密码还是不对。

杰克：我真的忘了，怎么办呢？

职员：您得再申请一个新的密码。请您填张表，签上名字，下个星期来取。

杰克：好。那我今天可以取钱吗？

职员：对不起，今天你取不了了，下个星期再来取吧。

问题

5. 杰克原来打算取什么钱？

6. 后来为什么不取了？

7. 杰克第一次填的是什么表？

8. 他为什么没有换到钱？

Lesson 34

听力练习 - Listening Practice

There are two listening materials in this section. Listen carefully and circle the correct answer to each question. Each listening material contains five questions.

Dialogue 1

　　玛丽(Mary)来到北京以后，买了不少明信片和手工艺品。那些明信片和手工艺品是要送给同学的。她还买了两套奥运会纪念品，奥运会就是奥林匹克(Olympic)运动会的意思。每套纪念品都有五个特别漂亮的小娃娃，他们的名字分别是：贝贝、晶晶、欢欢、迎迎、妮妮，连起来就是 "北京欢迎你"。来中国以前，玛丽在英国电视上看见过，玛丽的妹妹让她一定买一套送给她，还叫她一到北京就买。她到北京以后，找了好几家商店才发现了两套。她买下了那两套，她自己要留下一套。中国的旗袍也很漂亮，玛丽给妈妈买了一件。爸爸喜欢中国画儿，她给爸爸买了一幅中国画儿。爷爷奶奶都喜欢绣花睡衣，她给他们一人买了一套。东西买了不少，可是怎么寄回去呢？今天没有课，她想到邮局去问问怎么寄好。

问题

1. 玛丽给她同学买了什么？

2. 五个奥运娃娃的名字连起来是什么？

3. 她为什么买了两套娃娃？

4. 她给妈妈买了什么？

5. 她给爷爷买了什么？

Dialogue 2

玛丽：请问这儿可以寄包裹吗？

职员：当然可以，你想寄什么？

玛丽：我寄手工艺品和衣服。

职员：你得先买一个箱子，把你要寄的东西放进去，然后填一张表。

玛丽：这样行了吗？

职员：你还要把包裹打开，让我检查一下。

玛丽：好，请你检查。

职员：这瓶子里是什么？

玛丽：啊，我忘了告诉你了。这是药，是红花油，我爸爸常常背痛，他要我寄一瓶给他。

职员：那你得另外打一个包裹，红花油不能和这些东西一起寄。

玛丽：好。我把红花油拿出来。

职员：你要空运还是海运？

玛丽：海运吧，海运便宜一些，他们不等着用。

职员：好，请放在秤上。要保价吗？

玛丽：要保价！

职员：请付750块人民币，把箱子交给我就行了。

玛丽：好，谢谢，再见。

问题

6. 玛丽要先买一个什么？

7. 瓶子里面是什么东西？

8. 她爸爸有什么病？

9. 她为什么要海运？

10.保价是什么意思？

Lesson 35

听力练习- Listening Practice

There are two listening materials in this section. Listen carefully and circle the correct answer to each question. Each listening material contains four questions.

Dialogue 1

小王：小李，今天你怎么这么漂亮？头发都变了样。

小李：别提了！今天我快气死了。

小王：为什么？

小李：我到市中心的理发店理发，那个理发师把我的头发剪得这么短，还把我的头发染

成这个怪样子……

小王：你有没有搞错？如果你不同意，她能帮你剪吗？

小李：我同意她剪，也同意她染，可我没有叫她把我的头发剪成这样，染成这样。

小王：到底怎么回事？你能不能说清楚一点儿？

小李：是这样的。我一进理发店，那个理发师就给我洗头。她一边洗，一边说，现在很

流行剪短发，说我长得帅，剪成短发，一定和电影明星一样。

小王：那你就同意了？

小李：我就同意了。她就拿起剪子来剪，一剪子下去，我就知道剪得太短了。我说剪得

太短了。她说："你为什么不早说啊？现在剪下来了，接不上去了。"

小王：她说得对，那就是你的不是了。

小李：连你也这么说？！

问题

1. 小王为什么说小李今天很漂亮？

2. 小李为什么很生气？

3. 小李为什么同意理发师把头发剪短？

4. 小王说是谁的错？

Dialogue 2

小李：后来我只好让她剪了，她就把我剪成现在这个样子。

小王：还可以，不算难看。

小李：剪好了，那里的理发师都说，帅极了。他们还说，这种发型加上点红颜色才棒呢。

小王：你又同意了？

小李：我还没说"同意"，她已经给我染上了。

小王：原来你没有同意啊？！那你为什么不去找她的经理？

小李：找她经理干什么？

小王：告她，告她对顾客服务不好。

小李：不行啊。

小王：那为什么？她就是经理吗？

小李：不是，她是我朋友的妹妹。

小王：原来是这样！

　　　问题

5. 小李的头发被染成了什么颜色？

6. 谁说加上这种颜色才棒？

7. 为什么小李不去找经理？

8. 那个理发师是谁？

Lesson 36

听力练习 - Listening Practice

There are two listening materials in this section. Listen carefully and circle the correct answer to each question. Each listening material contains four questions.

Dialogue 1

我叫王为。我每天一大早就起来读汉语。因为我的妈妈是中国人，她要我学习中国文化，她把中国的文化都一一介绍给我和我的妹妹。她还要我们学习中国人早睡早起的好习惯，每天早上六点半我就起床。我同宿舍的同学马修和我不一样，他睡得很晚，起得也很晚。等我读完书，吃好早饭，已经是九点了，这时候他才起床。他没有时间吃早饭，天天如此。

今天我们有写作课。我读完书，吃完早饭，正准备去学校。看到我的朋友还在床上，我就对他说："马修，快起来，九点多了，你要迟到了！"可是马修说："今天十点有一场足球赛，我不想去上课了。你给我请一个假吧，就说我身体不舒服，怎么样？"我心里不同意，可是还是说"好。"

问题

1. 王为为什么习惯早睡早起？

2. 他起床后通常做什么？

3. 马修通常几点起床？

4. 马修为什么今天要请假？

Dialogue 2

老师：同学们早！

学生：老师早！

老师：今天为什么那么多同学没有来？

学生：老师，李健病了。他昨天在街上吃了一些北京小吃，今天早上拉肚子，我送他去医院，他住院了。他要我替他请假。

老师：天气热，吃东西要小心。我下课以后去医院看看他。大卫为什么没有来？

学生：他说他病了，感冒了，今天不能来上课。他说他向你请假了。

老师：我想起来了，他昨晚给我发了个短信。马修也感冒了吗？王为，你和他一个宿舍，你一定知道。

王为：老师，他要我给他请假，他说他不舒服。

老师：不舒服？ 我现在给他打个电话。我可以用一下你的手机吗？

王为：可以。

马修：喂，小王，比赛棒极了。现在是一比一。哎，你帮我请假了没有？

老师：马修，是我，张老师。我听说你病了，我借王为的手机给你打电话。

马修：张老师，真不好意思，我没病，我想看这场球赛……

老师：原来如此！这样很不好，你应该讲实话。

马修：对不起，张老师。我以后再也不这样了。我现在马上就去上课。

问题

5. 李健为什么没有来上课？

6. 李健现在在哪儿？

7. 大卫为什么没有来上课？

8. 老师怎么知道了马修没来上课的原因？

Lesson 37

听力练习- Listening Practice

There are two listening materials in this section. Listen carefully and circle the correct answer to each question. Each listening material contains four questions.

Dialogue 1

　　大明来到中国以后，游览了很多地方，他深深地爱上了中国的一切。前几天，他到山东旅游，住在一位大妈家里，他写信把这件事告诉爸爸妈妈了。大明的爸爸妈妈是中文老师，所以他用中文给爸爸妈妈写信。没想到妈妈接到信以后马上就来中国找他了。这到底是为什么呢？妈妈见到他以后赶紧问他："你还好吗？"他说："我没有病呀？！"妈妈说："身体没病，脑子是不是出了毛病？"大明说："怎么会呢？我很正常。""那你为什么和马一起住，一起吃草呢？"妈妈问他。原来大明写错字了，他把大妈写成了大马了，把菜写成草了。他在信里告诉爸爸妈妈，他每天跟大马一起到地里干活，一起吃新鲜草。这可把爸爸妈妈急坏了。

问题

1. 大明的爸爸妈妈做什么工作？

2. 大明前几天在哪儿旅游？

3. 为什么妈妈去中国找他？

4. 大明想写哪两个字？

Dialogue 2

邮递员：您早！

大明：您早！有我的信吗？

邮递员：信倒是没有，有一张明信片。

大明：明信片？谁寄给我的？

邮递员：你自己看看。

大明：啊，是从上海寄的，一定是我的朋友王京寄的。

邮递员：你再仔细看看。

大明：啊，这不是我寄出去的明信片吗？怎么又回来了？

邮递员：是啊，怎么又回来了？

大明：我没有把地址写错呀？！我特别注意把收信人的地址写在上面。

邮递员：对，地址没有写反。

大明：那到底是为什么？

邮递员：你不觉得上面少了点儿什么吗？

大明：什么也没少，我寄出去的时候就这样。

邮递员：我是说明信片上面应该有的东西，而你的上面没有。

大明：我真的看不出，请你告诉我吧。

邮递员：你没有贴邮票啊，先生！

问题

5. 大明收到了什么？

6. 是谁寄给他的？

7. 他信封上的地址是怎么写的？

8. 东西为什么又回来了？

Lesson 38

听力练习- Listening Practice

There are two listening materials in this section. Listen carefully and circle the correct answer to each question. Each listening material contains four questions.

Dialogue 1

马里来中国学习中文已经快一年了，最近，他想去找一个工作。他找工作的原因有两个：第一个，他要自食其力。什么是自食其力呢？自食其力就是自己靠自己生活，不要爸爸妈妈的钱。马里说："虽然我爸爸很有钱，他不让我去打工，可是我已经二十一岁了，我可以靠自己的两只手生存。" 他找工作的第二个原因是他想通过打工提高中文水平。他有很多英国朋友，英国朋友看到他都喜欢讲英语。他也有很多中国朋友，可是他们都想跟他练习英语，从来不跟他说汉语。他跟他们说过好几次，要他们说汉语，可是没有用，他们还是说英语，他也就不好意思再要求他们了。他想，只有去打工练习汉语了。他写信申请了几个单位，可是连一个面试的机会都没有。最近，他到一家合资公司去申请工作，他参加了面试。刚开始老板很高兴，说："你的汉语讲得很不错。" 可是，当他拿出他的简历时，老板改变了主意，让他回家听信，他很难过。

问题

1. 马里来中国多久了？

2. 他为什么要去打工？

3. 他为什么不能跟他的中国朋友练习汉语？

4. 他为什么没有被合资公司录用？

Dialogue 2

马里：嗨，没想到在中国找工作也这么难！

朋友：听你的口气，在英国找工作一定很不容易了。

马里：是啊，在英国找工作很不容易。一个工作，几十个人申请。

朋友：在中国是一个工作，几百个人申请。

马里：真的？普通的工作也是这样吗？

朋友：是啊，工资比较高的工作更是不得了。

马里：中国好像失业的人不多，大家都在工作。

朋友：没办法，总得吃饭啊！

马里：大学生找工作难不难？

朋友：说难也难，说不难也不难。有的人高不成低不就，所以很难找到工作。

马里：什么是高不成低不就？

朋友：就是差的工作他不想去，好的工作呢，人家不要他。

马里：哦。可是我不是高不成低不就，怎么我还是找不到工作呢？

朋友：简历也很重要。简历写得好，往往是成功的一半。

马里：我的工作经历不多，写来写去写不出东西来。

朋友：那你把求职信好好写一下，把你的爱好、能力都写出来。

马里：你帮我把求职信改一改，好不好？

朋友：没问题。我一定会把你推销出去的。

问题

5. 在英国，一个工作一般有多少人申请？

6. 在中国，一个工作一般有多少人申请？

7. 为什么有的大学生找不到工作？

8. 马里的朋友要帮助他修改什么？

Lesson 39

听力练习 - Listening Practice

There are two listening materials in this section. Listen carefully and circle the correct answer to each question. Each listening material contains four questions.

Dialogue 1

春节快到了！春节是中国人最大的也是最重要的节日。今年的春节是王力大学毕业以后的第一个春节。他上个月才找到了一个他喜欢的工作，现在的工资是三千元一个月。不仅如此，他还交了一个漂亮的女朋友。因为他一个人在这个大城市工作，所以他的女朋友请他去她家过年，这真是喜上加喜，他高兴极了。今天是星期天，一大早，他的女朋友就来找他一起去南京路买东西。南京路上人来人往，每家店里都是人山人海。他问他的女朋友：“你爸爸妈妈喜欢什么东西？”他女朋友说，不管什么，只要是我们买的，他们都会喜欢的。她还说：“爸爸妈妈知道你刚开始工作，没有多少钱，有个礼物意思意思就行了。”可是王力说，第一次见面，一定要送个贵重的礼物，礼物轻了就是对老人不尊重。正说着，他看到了一件适合老人的礼物，他刚要买，却发现他的钱包不见了……

问题

1. 王力每月的工资是多少？

2. 为什么说王力这个春节是喜上加喜？

3. 他们去南京路给谁买礼物？

4. 他为什么没有买？

Dialogue 2

王力：嗨，我的钱包不见了。

女友：真的？！你是不是忘带了？

王力：肯定带了，我出门的时候检查过了。

女友：刚才我看到有个十几岁的孩子在我们身边，会不会是他偷的？

王力：哪一个小孩？

女友：就是那一个！

王力：喂，你，你刚才是不是偷了我的钱包？

女友：我看到你一直在我们的身边。

小孩：放开我，你们在说什么呀？

王力：你偷了我的钱包。

小孩：我没有偷什么钱包，我从来不偷东西！

女友：你把钱包交出来吧，不然我们要报警了。

小孩：你的钱包是什么样的？你认得出你的钱包吗？

女友：当然认得出！瞧，警察来了。警察，我们抓到了一个小偷！

王力：他偷了我的钱包，我们把他抓住了。

警察：等一等，你是说你的钱包不见了？

王力：是的，我的钱包不见了。刚才他就在我们旁边。

警察：这孩子不是小偷。他看到一个小偷就报告了我们。我们把小偷抓住了。这个小偷
偷了好几个钱包，你们看看，哪个是你们的？

王力：这个是。钱也没有少。对不起，我们错怪了这孩子。

女友：对不起，真不好意思。谢谢你。

小孩：不谢，再见。警察叔叔再见。

问题

5. 王力什么时候检查了钱包？

6. 为什么他们以为是那个孩子偷了钱包？

7. 警察为什么不抓那个孩子？

8. 那个小孩做了什么好事？

Lesson 40

听力练习- Listening Practice

There are two listening materials in this section. Listen carefully and circle the correct answer to each question. Each listening material contains four questions.

Dialogue 1

查理是个足球运动员，他的身体很棒。他常常到世界各地旅游，爬山是他最喜爱的活动。今年他有机会到中国参加足球比赛，他高兴极了，因为他一直都想来中国。这次，他比其他队员提前两天到达北京。刚到北京，他一放下行李就立刻去参观了天安门和故宫。第二天，他就上了长城。他早就听说毛主席说过"不到长城非好汉"，所以他一定要当上好汉。他站在长城上，照了好几张相。他把相片寄回家，还打电话告诉他爸爸妈妈说："现在我登上了长城，可以算一个好汉了！"他爸爸妈妈听了非常高兴，说："我们明年夏天一定也去当一次好汉。"

问题

1. 查理最喜欢做什么？

2. 他来中国做什么？

3. 下面这些地点，查理哪个没去？

4. 查理的爸爸妈妈明年来中国干什么？

Dialogue 2

爸爸：谢谢你，王京。这些日子你给我们当向导，真是帮了我们的大忙。

王京：哪儿的话，儿子为父母做事是应该的。

妈妈：没想到我儿子懂事多了，给爸爸妈妈做事不要钱了。

王京：我在中国学到了不少东西。对不起妈妈，我以前不该要你们的钱。

爸爸：没什么，不同的地方有不同的文化。你在英国干活拿钱是应该的。

妈妈：我倒是喜欢中国文化，你帮我，我帮你，不要太计较。

王京：可是中国正在改变，有些年轻人觉得西方的观念好，也开始计较了。

妈妈：我注意到了。服务员很在意小费。

爸爸：人家给你服务，给人家小费是应该的。

妈妈：王京，要陪我们去西安的那位姑娘，你看我们应该给她多少小费？

王京：妈妈，你不用管了，我来处理就行了。

爸爸：虽然她是你的好朋友，可是我们也不能白用人家。

王京：爸，你就别管了，她很想认识你们呢。

爸爸：想认识我们？她是不是在追你？

妈妈：谁追谁还说不定呢！

王京：你们搞错了，她只是我的一个普通朋友，她是我同班同学李明的妹妹。

问题

5. 为什么妈妈说王京懂事了？

6. 王京从中国学到了什么？

7. 王京的爸爸妈妈明天要去哪儿？

8. 谁陪他们去？

附录三 **Appendix 3**　汉字笔顺 **Stroke Order**　lesson 31

读	、	讠	订	讣	诗	诗	诗	读	读	读			
注	、	丶	氵	沪	汻	泞	汪	注					
册	丿	刀	刑	册	册								
如	乀	夂	女	女	如	如							
修	丿	亻	仁	仃	俏	俏	修	修	修				
取	一	厂	厅	耵	耳	耳	取	取					
健	丿	亻	们	伊	侓	侓	律	健	健				
思	丶	冂	曰	囲	田	田	思	思	思				
量	丶	丿	尸	吊	旦	旱	昌	昌	昌	昌	量	量	
格	一	十	才	木	杉	柊	柊	格	格				
订	、	讠	订	订									
办	丿	力	办	办									
续	乚	纟	纟	纩	纩	统	统	结	续	续			
钥	丿	左	左	钅	铲	钔	钥	钥	钥				
匙	丿	丌	旧	日	旦	早	早	异	是	是	匙		
科	丿	二	千	手	禾	禾	科	科					
数	丶	丷	粃	米	米	米	娄	娄	数	数	数	数	
杂	丿	九	九	杂	杂	杂							
志	一	十	士	士	志	志	志						
阅	、	丨	门	门	闩	闩	阅	阅	阅	阅			
览	丶	丨	虴	虴	呰	览	览	览					
设	、	讠	订	设	设	设							
般	’	丿	丿	舟	舟	舟	舟	舡	船	般			
约	乚	纟	纟	纩	约	约							

选	`	⌐	牛	生	步	先	⅛先	选	选					
目	l	冂	月	目	目									
武	一	二	干	下	示	正	武	武						
术	一	十	才	木	术									
兵	一	⌐	⌐	斤	丘	兵								
兵	`	⌐	⌐	斤	丘	兵								
活	`	`	氵	汗	汗	汗	活	活	活					
队	了	阝	阝	队										
私	一	二	千	禾	禾	私	私							
证	`	讠	证	订	证	证	证							
死	一	厂	歹	歹	歹	死								
每	`	⌐	仁	每	每	每	每							
迟	`	刁	尸	尺	沢	识	迟							
部	`	二	立	立	立	音	音	部	部					
身	`	亻	勹	身	身	身	身							
体	ノ	亻	仁	什	仹	休	体							
俱	ノ	亻	们	仃	仴	但	俱	俱	俱	俱				
锻	ノ	⅛	钅	钅	钅	钌	钌	锉	锉	锻	锻	锻	锻
炼	`	`	丬	火	灯	炉	炼	炼	炼					
棒	一	十	才	木	杆	杆	杛	棒	楱	棒	棒	棒	
仅	ノ	亻	仅	仅										
而	一	⌐	厂	丙	而	而								
且	l	冂	月	且	且									
改	`	刁	己	己	改	改	改							

lesson 33

职	一	厂	卄	耵	耳	耵	职	职	职	职	
账	丨	冂	刀	贝	贝丿	贝二	账	账			
往	丿	彳	彳	彳	往	往	往	往			
份	丿	亻	亻	份	份	份					
奖	丶	丬	丬	籵	籵	籵	籵	奖	奖		
存	一	ナ	才	存	存	存					
另	丶	口	口	号	另						
较	一	七	车	车	轫	轫	轫	轫	较	较	
货	丿	亻	化	化	化	货	货	货			
管	丿	竹	竹	竹	竹	竹	竹	笢	筶	筶	管 管
联	一	厂	卄	耵	耳	耳	耳	耴	耴	联	联
际	阝	阝	阝	阡	阡	阡	际				
香	一	二	千	禾	禾	禾	香	香	香		
港	丶	氵	氵	汇	汇	洪	洪	洪	洪	港	港
丢	一	二	千	王	丢	丢					
盗	丶	冫	冫	次	次	次	次	盗	盗	盗	
址	一	十	圵	圵	址	址	址				
单	丶	丷	丷	单	单	单	单				
密	丶	丷	宀	宀	宓	宓	密	密	密	密	
旧	丨	丨丨	旧	旧	旧						
处	丿	夂	夂	处	处						
列	一	歹	歹	歹	列	列					
透	一	二	千	禾	秀	秀	秀	诱	透		
标	一	十	才	木	杤	杤	标	标	标		

裹	亠	亠	亠	亩	亩	查	衷	表	裹	裹	裹	裹
绣	ㄥ	ㄥ	纟	纟	纟	纤	纤	绣	绣			
套	一	大	大	太	本	本	套	套	套	套		
按	一	扌	扌	扩	扩	护	按	按	按			
规	一	二	丰	夫	却	却	规	规				
必	丶	心	心	必	必							
须	丿	彡	彡	彡	彡	须	须	须				
检	一	十	才	木	杧	杧	检	检	检	检		
或	一	一	戸	口	豆	或	或	或				
称	丿	二	千	禾	禾	利	称	称	称	称		
纪	ㄥ	ㄥ	纟	纟	纪	纪						
念	丿	人	亼	今	今	念	念	念				
邮	丶	口	曰	由	由	由	邮					
局	一	一	尸	月	吊	局	局					
属	一	一	尸	尸	尸	居	居	尼	属	属	属	
阳	阝	阝	阝	阳	阳	阳						
原	一	厂	厂	尸	厏	厏	盾	原	原	原		
轮	一	七	车	车	轩	轮	轮	轮				
输	一	七	车	车	轩	轮	轮	轮	输	输	输	输
平	一	一	灭	平	平							
价	丿	亻	亻	价	价	价						
询	丶	讠	讠	讠	询	询	询					
赔	丨	口	贝	贝	贝	贮	贮	贮	赔	赔	赔	
偿	丿	亻	亻	亻	偿	偿	偿	偿	偿	偿		

lesson 35

型	一	二	于	开	刑	刑	刑	型	型				
廊	、	亠	广	广	庐	庐	庐	庶	廊	廊			
剪	、	丷	丷	产	前	前	前	前	剪	剪			
吹	丶	口	口	叩	吹	吹	吹						
士	一	十	士										
烫	、	冫	氵	汙	汤	汤	汤	烫	烫				
染	、	冫	氵	氿	沈	氿	染	染	染				
排	一	丁	扌	扛	扣	抈	排	排	排	排			
显	丶	口	曰	曰	旦	昻	昻	昻	显				
引	ˊ	ㄱ	弓	引									
短	丿	广	上	乍	矢	矢	知	知	知	知	短	短	
板	一	十	才	木	朾	扳	板	板					
寸	一	寸	寸										
帅	丨	刂	帅	帅	帅								
精	丶	丷	丷	斗	半	米	米	米	粘	粘	精	精	精
神	丶	宀	礻	礻	衧	初	初	初	神				
洗	丶	冫	氵	汇	汇	沪	洸	洗					
于	一	二	于										
府	丶	一	广	广	庁	庁	府	府					
井	一	二	圭	井									
街	丶	丿	彳	彳	扑	往	往	往	往	往	街	街	
宾	丶	丷	宀	宀	宁	宁	宾	宾	宾				
顾	一	厂	厉	厄	厄	厄	厄	顾	顾	顾			
之	、	冫	之										

羊	、	丷	丷	ⵙ	兰	羊						
拉	一	十	扌	扩	扩	拉	拉					
替	一	二	丰	夫	夫	麸	麸	麸	替	替	替	
例	丿	亻	亻	伫	伪	伪	例	例				
抄	一	十	扌	扏	扪	抄	抄					
签	丿	𠂉	𥫗	𥫗	𥫗	竹	梦	笅	签	签	签	签
己	𠃌	𠃍	己									
同	丨	冂	冂	同	同	同						
笨	丿	𠂉	𥫗	𥫗	𥫗	竹	竿	笨	笨	笨		
聪	一	𠃊	耳	耳	耳	耳	耵	聊	聊	聪	聪	聪
讲	、	讠	讲	讲	讲	讲						
范	一	艹	艹	艹	范	范	范	范				
围	丨	冂	冂	同	同	围	围					
内	丨	冂	内	内								
告	丿	丄	牛	生	牛	告	告					
诉	、	讠	讠	诉	诉	诉	诉					
区	一	𠃍	又	区								
紧	一	𝆐	竹	収	坚	坚	坚	紧	紧			
急	丿	𠂊	刍	刍	刍	急	急	急	急			
尊	丷	丷	丷	酋	酋	酋	酋	酋	尊	尊	尊	
敬	一	十	艹	艹	芍	芍	苟	苟	苟	敬	敬	敬
此	丨	𠄌	止	此	此	此						
致	一	工	至	至	至	至	致	致	致			
将	、	丬	丬	丬	㢩	将	将	将	将			

lesson 37

退	コ	ヨ	ヨ	艮	艮	艮	艮	退	退			
封	一	十	土	圭	丰	圭	圭	封	封			
反	一	厂	厅	反								
啦	丨	口	口	口	叶	啦	吤	吤	吤	啦	啦	
靠	丿	丄	牛	生	告	告	告	告	靠	靠	靠	靠
阿	了	阝	阝	阿	阿	阿	阿					
伯	丿	亻	亻	佔	伯	伯	伯					
达	一	大	大	达	达	达						
裙	丶	ネ	ネ	ネ	ネ	衤	衤	衤	裙	裙	裙	
辫	丶	ン	二	亍	立	立	辛	辛	辛	辛	辫	
世	一	十	廿	世	世							
界	丶	口	口	田	田	甼	界	界	界			
亲	丶	立	立	立	立	辛	辛	亲				
切	一	七	切	切								
误	丶	讠	讠	讦	讦	误	误	误				
获	一	十	艹	艹	犷	犷	获	获	获			
全	丿	人	今	全	全	全						
惯	丶	忄	忄	忄	忄	忄	惯	惯	惯	惯	惯	
居	一	尸	尸	尸	屑	屑	居	居				
食	丿	人	仝	今	今	含	食	食	食			
伙	丿	亻	亻	仦	伙	伙						
伴	丿	亻	亻	亻	伴	伴	伴					
祝	丶	ネ	ネ	ネ	ネ	礻	祀	祀	祝			
康	丶	广	广	庐	庐	序	序	庚	康	康		

招	一	寸	扌	护	护	招	招					
聘	一	厂	打	耵	月	耳	耵	耴	聃	聃	聘	聘
实	丶	宀	宀	宊	宊	实	实					
者	一	十	土	耂	耂	者	者					
资	丶	冫	欠	汐	次	次	次	咨	资	资		
众	丿	人	个	仌	众	众						
瓜	一	厂	爪	瓜	瓜							
夸	一	大	大	太	夻	夸						
推	一	扌	扌	扩	打	抃	抃	抃	推	推		
销	丿	亻	卜	钅	钅	钊	钊	钋	销	销	销	
毕	一	亻	上	比	比	毕						
皇	丿	亻	白	白	白	皀	皇	皇	皇			
苏	一	艹	艹	芐	芀	苏	苏					
兰	丶	丷	丛	兰	兰	兰						
悉	丿	宀	宀	平	平	采	采	采	悉	悉	悉	
胜	丿	月	月	月	月	胪	胪	胖	胜			
任	丿	亻	仁	仁	仟	任						
籍	竹	竹	竿	竿	箁	箁	籍	籍	籍	籍	籍	
传	丿	亻	亻	仁	传	传						
至	一	工	云	玄	至	至						
龄	丨	卜	止	此	止	步	齿	齿	齿	龄	龄	龄
建	一	曰	彐	彐	聿	聿	建	建				
筑	丿	竹	竹	竹	竹	竿	竿	筝	筑	筑	筑	
技	一	寸	扌	扩	技	技						

lesson 39

陪	了	阝	阝`	阝	阼	阼	陪	陪	陪				
购	丿	冂	贝	贝	贝	购	购	购					
逛	丿	犭	犭	犭	犴	狂	狂	狂	逛	逛			
随	了	阝	阝一	阝	阼	阼	陌	陌	随	随			
膏	丶	亠	广	六	亩	亩	高	高	高	高	亭	膏	膏	膏
刷	乛	乛	尸	尸	刁	刷	刷	刷					
肥	丿	刀	月	月	肝	肥	肥	肥					
皂	丶	亻	白	白	白	皂	皂						
齐	丶	亠	六	文	文	齐							
与	一	与	与										
其	一	十	廿	廿	甘	其	其	其					
由	丶	冂	口	由	由								
廉	丶	亠	广	广	产	产	庐	庐	庐	庩	廉	廉	廉
万	一	丆	万										
洞	丶	冫	氵	汩	洞	洞	洞	洞	洞				
故	一	十	古	古	古	盐	故	故					
骗	乛	马	马	马丶	驴	驴	驴	骗	骗	骗	骗		
姑	〈	女	女	女	姑	妊	姑	姑					
娘	〈	女	女	女	妒	妒	娘	娘	娘				
追	丶	㇇	乞	户	白	自	自	泊	追				
优	丿	亻	亻	仕	优	优							
惠	一	亠	一	向	百	車	車	車	惠	惠	惠		
折	一	扌	扌	扩	扩	折	折						
骂	丶	丶	马	马	骂	骂	骂	骂					

宫	、	ハ	宀	宀	帘	宫	宫	宫				
博	一	十	忄	忄	忄	恒	恒	博	博	博	博	
观	フ	又	䅏	䅏	观	观						
安	、	丷	宀	宊	安	安						
止	丨	卜	止	止								
访	、	讠	讠	讠	访	访						
举	、	丷	丷	兴	兴	兴	兴	举				
宴	、	丷	宀	宀	宀	宔	宴	宴	宴			
主	、	二	二	丰	主							
席	、	一	广	广	庐	庐	庐	庐	席	席		
堂	丨	丷	丷	丷	尚	尚	堂	堂	堂	堂		
仪	丿	亻	仁	仪	仪							
束	一	一	一	申	申	束	束					
何	丿	亻	仁	仁	何	何	何					
禁	一	十	才	木	村	村	材	林	林	禁	禁	禁	禁
景	一	冂	冂	日	旦	旦	旯	畧	畧	景	景	景
帝	、	二	亠	亠	产	产	帝	帝				
占	丨	卜	卜	占	占							
米	、	丷	丷	半	米	米						
模	木	杧	杧	栉	栉	栉	横	横	模	模		
古	一	十	十	古	古							
群	フ	刁	刁	尹	尹	君	君	君	君	群	群	群	群
微	丿	彳	彳	彳	微	微	微	微	微	微	微	微
入	丿	入										

附录四 Appendix 4

拼音文本　Pinyin Text to Dialogues and Reading

Warming up Lesson

Dialogue One

Xuésheng:	Shīfu, wǒ qù Běijīng Yǔyán Dàxué.
Shīfu:	Hǎo. Nǐ de xíngli zhème duō, xiǎo xiāngzi fàng zài dà xiāngzi shang, kěyǐ ma?
Xuésheng:	Dà xiāngzi lǐmiàn yǒu píngzi, xiǎoxīn bié bǎ píngzi nòngpò le.
Shīfu:	Chē hòubèixiāng kǒngpà zhuāng bú xià le.
Xuésheng:	Nà bǎ xiǎo xiāngzi fàng zài wǒ pángbiān de zuòwèi shang ba.
Shīfu:	Hǎo. Shàng chē ba.
Xuésheng:	Xièxie.
Shīfu:	Nǐ shì lái shàng xué de ba?
Xuésheng:	Duì, wǒ lái xué yì nián Zhōngwén.
Shīfu:	Nǐ shì nǎ guó rén?
Xuésheng:	Yíxiàzi shuō bu qīngchu. Wǒ bàba shì Fǎguórén, wǒ māma shì Déguórén.
Shīfu:	Nǐ shì zài nǎr chūshēng de?
Xuésheng:	Déguó. Búguò yī suì shí wǒ jiù qùle Fǎguó, wǒ shì zài Fǎguó zhǎngdà de.
Shīfu:	Nǐ shì zài nǎr shàng de xué?
Xuésheng:	Xiǎoxué shì zài Fǎguó shàng de, zhōngxué hé dàxué shì zài Yīngguó shàng de.
Shīfu:	Nǐ ná de shì nǎ guó hùzhào?
Xuésheng:	Wǒ yǒu liǎng běn hùzhào, yì běn shì Fǎguó de, yì běn shì Yīngguó de.
Shīfu:	Nà nǐ zhǐ néng shuō shì Ōuzhōurén le.
Xuésheng:	Duì, wǒ shì Ōuzhōurén, Xī'ōurén.

Dialogue Two

Xuésheng:	Shīfu, Běijīng de jiāotōng zǒngshì zhème yōngjǐ ma?
Shīfu:	Jīntiān hái kěyǐ, yǒu shíhou gèng yōngjǐ.
Xuésheng:	Zhēn méi xiǎngdào Běijīng yǒu zhème duō qìchē, gēn Lúndūn chàbuduō.
Shīfu:	Xiànzài yǒu qián de rén duō le, yǒu qìchē de rén yě jiù duō le.
Xuésheng:	Wǒ tīngshuō Zhōngguó shì zìxíngchē de wángguó, shàng-xiàbān shí rénmen dōu qí zìxíngchē.
Shīfu:	Nà shì guòqù. Xiànzài kāichē de, zuò dìtiě de, zuò gōnggòng qìchē de, zuò bānchē de, dǎdí de, qí zìxíngchē de, shénmeyàng de dōu yǒu.
Xuésheng:	Shīfu, Běijīng qìchē jìn chéng yào bu yào jiāo jìnchéngfèi?

Shīfu:	Bú yòng. Tīngshuō Lúndūn jìn chéng yào jiāo wǔ bàng qián, shì ma?
Xuésheng:	Xiànzài zhǎng le, yào jiāo bā bàng le.
Shīfu:	Tài duō le! Yì tiān bā Yīngbàng, hé Rénmínbì yì bǎi duō kuài qián ne.
Xuésheng:	Duō shì duō, kěshì xiànzài kāichē shàngbān de rén shǎo le, jiāotōng hǎo duō le.
Shīfu:	Chūzūchē sījǐ zěnmebàn? Tāmen tiāntiān zài chéng li kāi chē, yě yào jiāo qián ma?
Xuésheng:	Hǎoxiàng tāmen bú yòng jiāo.
Shīfu:	Zhè hái chàbuduō.

Text

Huàr Shì Shuí Tōu De?

Zhāng xiānsheng shì ge jǐngchá. Zhè tiān wǎnshang, tā jiēdàole yí ge diànhuà, tīng bù qīng shuōhuà rén de shēngyīn, zhǐ tīngdào yǒu rén shuō: Měishùguǎn (art gallery) de mínghuàr bèi tōu le. Tā fàngxià diànhuà hòu mǎshàng qùle měishùguǎn. Měishùguǎn li yǒu liǎng ge gōngzuò rényuán, yí ge shì shàng zǎobān de, yí ge shì shàng wǎnbān de. Zhāng Xiānsheng wèn tāmen: "Shì shuí fāxiàn huàr bèi tōu le?" Shàng wǎnbān de shuō: "Shì tā gāngcái gàosu wǒ de." Zhāng xiānsheng jiù wèn shàng zǎobān de: "Nǐ shì shénme shíhou fāxiàn huàr bèi tōu de?" Shàng zǎobān de shuō: "Jiù zài gāngcái. Wǒ liǎng ge xiǎoshí qián guānmén de shíhou huàr hái zài. Huíjiā de lùshang wǒ xiǎng qǐlái yǒu jiàn dōngxi wàng zài bàngōngshì le, suǒyǐ yòu huílái le. Dào le zhèr yǐhòu, wǒ fāxiàn huàr bú jiàn le." Zhè shí Zhāng xiānsheng yòu wèn: "Nǐmen rènwéi (think) huàr shì shuí tōu de ne?" Shàng zǎobān de rén shuō: "Bù zhīdao shì shuí dǎ de diànhuà. Tā yídìng gēn tōu huàr de rén yǒu guānxi." Zhāng xiānsheng shuō: "Nǐ shuō de duì. Wǒ zhīdào shì shuí tōu de le."

Lesson 31   Registering at a university

Dialogue One

Xuésheng:	Qǐngwèn, dú Zhōngwén de shì zài zhèr bàodào ma?
Lǎoshī:	Rúguǒ nǐ dú xuéwèi, qǐng dào Zhōngwénxì bàodào.
Xuésheng:	Wǒ bù dú xuéwèi, wǒ shì lái jìnxiū de.
Lǎoshī:	Nà nǐ zhǎo duì dìfang le, jìnxiū de jiù shì zài zhèr dēngjì zhùcè.
Xuésheng:	Xièxie! Zhè shì wǒ de lùqǔ tōngzhīshū hé hùzhào.
Lǎoshī:	Nǐ de Yīngwén míngzi jiào Jay Lee, Zhōngwén míngzi jiào Lǐ Jiàn, hěn yǒuyìsi.
Xuésheng:	Zhè ge míngzi shì wǒ de Zhōngwén lǎoshī gěi wǒ qǐ de, wǒ hěn xǐhuan.
Lǎoshī:	Búcuò, hěn yǒu lìliàng. Qǐng nǐ tiánxiě yíxià zhè zhāng biǎogé.
Xuésheng:	Yòng Zhōngwén tián háishi yòng Yīngwén tián?
Lǎoshī:	Rúguǒ nǐ néng yòng Zhōngwén tián, nà jiù yòng Zhōngwén tián.
Xuésheng:	Hǎo de. Lǎoshī, wǒ hái yùdìng le liúxuéshēng sùshè.
Lǎoshī:	Bànlǐ wán dēngjì shǒuxù yǐhòu, dào duìmiàn de bàngōngshì qù jiāo fèi lǐngqǔ yàoshi.
Xuésheng:	Xièxie.

Dialogue Two

Wáng Xiǎomíng:	Nǐ hǎo! Wǒ jiào Wáng Xiǎomíng, lái zì Mǎláixīyà.
Lǐ Jiàn:	Nǐ hǎo! Wǒ jiào Lǐ Jiàn, lái zì Yīngguó.
Wáng Xiǎomíng:	Wǒ jiù zhù zài nǐ duìmiàn, 325 hào fángjiān.
Lǐ Jiàn:	Nǐ yě shì lái dú yǔyán de ma?
Wǎng Xiǎomíng:	Bù, wǒ shì lái dú lǐkē de, wǒ dú shùxué.
Lǐ Jiàn:	Nǐ qùguo xuéxiào de túshūguǎn méiyǒu? Wǒ xiǎng qù jiè běn zázhì kànkan.
Wáng Xiǎomíng:	Xuéxiào yǒu wénkē hé lǐkē liǎng ge túshūguǎn, wǒ zhǐ qùguo lǐkē túshūguǎn.
Lǐ Jiàn:	Túshūguǎn de shèbèi zěnmeyàng?
Wáng Xiǎomíng:	Hěn xiānjìn, yǒu hěn duō jìsuànjī, hái yǒu kōngtiáo.
Lǐ Jiàn:	Yuèlǎnshì dà bu dà?
Wáng Xiǎomíng:	Hěn dà. Búguò rén hěn duō, nǐ yào zǎo qù, bùrán jiù méiyǒu zuòwèi le.
Lǐ Jiàn:	Zhēn de ?! Nà wǒ děi zǒu le. Huítóu jiàn.
Wáng Xiǎomíng:	Huítóu jiàn.

Text

Qù Zhōngguó Xuéxí Hànyǔ

Rúguǒ nǐ xiǎng qù Zhōngguó xuéxí Hànyǔ, nǐ yào xiān zhǎo hǎo xuéxiào. Zhōngguó hěn duō dàxué dōu kāishè duìwài Hànyǔ kè, yǒude zài Hànyǔxì, yǒude zài yǔyán zhōngxīn. Měi nián dōu yǒu dàliàng de wàiguó liúxuéshēng dào Zhōngguó de dàxué xuéxí Hànyǔ.

Kāishǐ shàng kè yǐqián, nǐ yào xiān cānjiā fēnbān kǎoshì. Chūjí bān wéi língqǐdiǎn, yìdiǎnr Hànyǔ dōu bú huì de tóngxué yě kěyǐ cānjiā. Zhōngjí bān de tóngxué xūyào zhǎngwò bābǎi dào yìqiān. ge hànzì, bìngqiě néng yòng Hànyǔ jìnxíng jiāotán. Gāojí bān de tóngxué zhìshǎo xūyào rènshi yìqiān wǔbǎi ge Hànzì, hái yào néng dúdǒng Zhōngwén bàozhǐ, kàndǒng Zhōngwén diànshì jiémù. Chū-zhōng-gāojí bān gè bān rénshù tōngcháng zài èrshí rén zuǒyòu.

Zhōngguó de xuéxiào yìbān shàngwǔ bā diǎn kāishǐ shàng kè, shí'èr diǎn chī wǔfàn, zhōngwǔ xiūxi liǎng ge xiǎoshí, xiàwǔ liǎng diǎn yòu kāishǐ shàng kè. Měi zhōu shàng kè de shíjiān dàyuē wéi èrshí ge xiǎoshí. Zhōngguó de dàxué yì nián fēnwéi liǎng ge xuéqī, měi nián de Jiǔ yuè chū hé Èr yuè dǐ kāi xué. Měi ge xuéqī de xuéxí shíjiān wéi shíliù dào èrshí zhōu. Xuéxiào yìbān dōu yǒu liúxuéshēng sùshè, sùshè lǐmiàn yǒu diànshì, diànhuà, kōngtiáo, bīngxiāng děng shèshī, liúxuéshēng dàduō xǐhuan zhù zài xiàoyuán li.

Lesson 32   Selecting a course

Dialogue One

Xiǎo Lǐ:	Nín hǎo! Wǒ xiǎng xuǎnxiū Zhōngguó gōngfukè, kěshì mùlù shang méiyǒu.
Lǎoshī:	Yǒu, nǐ kàn, zài zhèr.
Xiǎo Lǐ:	Wǔshù jiù shì gōngfu ma?
Lǎoshī:	Duì, wǔshù shì xuémíng.
Xiǎo Lǐ:	Wǒ míngbai le, xièxie.
Lǎoshī:	Wǔshù kè yì zhōu yí cì, Xīngqī'èr xiàwǔ sān diǎn dào sì diǎn.
Xiǎo Lǐ:	Xīngqī'èr xiàwǔ wǒ yǒu pīngpāngqiú huódòng.
Lǎoshī:	Zhème qiǎo, nǐ shì xiàoduì duìyuǎn ma?
Xiǎo Lǐ:	Bú shì, wǒ gānggāng kāishǐ xué, qǐngle ge sīrén jiàoliàn.
Lǎoshī:	Nà nǐ gēn jiàoliàn shāngliang yíxià, kànkan néng bu néng huàn ge shíjiān.
Xiǎo Lǐ:	Hǎo. Wǒ cóng xiǎo jiù xǐhuan Zhōngguó gōngfu, wǒ yídìng yào xuǎnxiū zhè mén kè.
Lǎoshī:	Nà nǐ kěyǐ xiànzài zhùcè. Nǐ dài xuéshēngzhèng le ma?
Xiǎo Lǐ:	Wǒ de xuéshēngzhèng hái méiyǒu bànhǎo, wǒ hái méi pāi zhàopiàn ne.
Lǎoshī:	Dàtīng li jiù yǒu zìdòng zhàoxiàngjī, qiáo, jiù zài nàbiān!
Xiǎo Lǐ:	Wǒ kàndào le, zhēn shì tài fāngbiàn le, Wǒ xiànzài jiù qù pāi. Xièxie!
Lǎoshī:	Búkèqi.

Dialogue Two

Xiǎo Fāng:	Xiǎo Lǐ, wǒ kuài yào lèisǐ le, měi zhōu yào shàng 18 jié kè.
Xiǎo Lǐ:	Nà wǒ jiù gèng bú yòng huó le, wǒ yào shàng 22 jié, érqiě dàbùfen dōu zài shàngwǔ.
Xiǎo Fāng:	Wǒ de yě shì. Tiāntiān zǎoshang 8 diǎn jiù yǒu kè.
Xiǎo Lǐ:	Wǒ yǐjīng chídào liǎng cì le, zhēn yǒudiǎn bù hǎo yìsi.
Xiǎo Fāng:	Wèntí shì zhèli chídào de rén hěn shǎo, dàjiā dōu hěn zìjué.
Xiǎo Lǐ:	Nǐ hái xuǎnxiūle biéde kè ma?
Xiǎo Fāng:	Xuǎn le, Zhōngguó shūfǎ hé Tàijíquán. Nǐ ne?
Xiǎo Lǐ:	Wǒ cānjiāle jiànshēn jùlèbù, xiàwǔ wǒ yào qù jiànshēnfáng duànliàn.
Xiǎo Fāng:	Xuéxiào li yǒu jiànshēnfáng ma?
Xiǎo Lǐ:	Bùjǐn yǒu, érqiě hěn bàng.
Xiǎo Fāng:	Zhēn de? Wǒ hái yǐwéi Zhōngguórén zhǐ xǐhuan dǎ pīngpāngqiú ne.
Xiǎo Lǐ:	Tāmen shénme qiú dōu xǐhuan.
Xiǎo Fāng:	Shì ma? Tāmen hǎoxiàng bù xǐhuan dǎ bàngqiú.
Xiǎo Lǐ:	Bú shì bù xǐhuan, ér shì méiyǒu chǎngdì.

Text

Xīn De Shēnghuó Fāngshì

Xiànzài zài Zhōngguó, jiànshēn fēicháng liúxíng. Nánnǚlǎoshào dōu hěn xǐhuan jiànshēn. Lǎoniánrén yìbān xǐhuan mànpǎo, dǎ Tàijíquán hé tiàowǔ. Zài chéngshì li, měi tiān zǎoshang nǐ dōu huì kàndào hěn duō lǎoniánrén dào gōngyuán qù, xiān mànpǎo jǐ fēnzhōng, ránhòu dǎdǎ Tàijíquán. Xiàtiān de wǎnshang, tāmen chángcháng láidào guǎngchǎng, hé péngyoumen yìqǐ tiàowǔ duànliàn shēntǐ. Tāmen dōu juéde kāishǐ duànliàn yǐhòu, shēntǐ bǐ yǐqián hǎoduō le. Xiànzài duànliàn yǐjīng chéngle tāmen shēnghuó zhōng zhòngyào de yíbùfen.

Zuìjìn jǐ nián lái, zài dà chéngshì li dàochù dōu kěyǐ jiàndào jiànshēnfáng, qīngniánrén dōu hěn xǐhuan qù jiànshēnfáng duànliàn. Duànliàn wán yǐhòu kěyǐ zài nàli hé péngyou huìmiàn, hē bēi kāfēi. Yǒu de rén rènwéi jiànshēn shì wèile duànliàn shēntǐ, kěshì yǒu de rén rènwéi jiànshēn bù jǐnjǐn shì wèile duànliàn shēntǐ, jiànshēn hái kěyǐ gǎibiàn yí ge rén de shēnghuó fāngshì. Zhè shì yì zhǒng xīn de shēnghuó fāngshì.

Lesson 33   At a bank

Dialogue One

Dà Wèi:	Nǐ hǎo! Wǒ xiǎng kāi yí ge pǔtōng de wǎnglái zhànghù.
Zhíyuán:	Dài shēnfènzhèng le méiyǒu ?
Dà Wèi:	Wǒ méiyǒu shēnfènzhèng, wǒ dàile hùzhào.
Zhíyuán:	Hùzhào yě kěyǐ. Nǐ yǒu jiǎngxuéjīn ma?
Dà Wèi:	Wǒ bú shì xuésheng, wǒ zài zhèr gōngzuò.
Zhíyuán:	Duìbuqǐ. Nǐ zài nǎ ge gōngsī gōngzuò?
Dà Wèi:	Kěkǒukělè gōngsī.
Zhíyuán:	Nǐ měi yuè dǎsuan cún duōshao qián?
Dà Wèi:	Liǎngwàn kuài zuǒyòu.
Zhíyuán:	Huóqī zhànghù lìxī bǐjiào dī, nǐ lìngwài zài kāi yí ge dìngqī zhànghù ba.
Dà Wèi:	Shénme shì huóqī, shénme shì dìngqī?
Zhíyuán:	Huóqī jiù shì wǎnglái zhànghù, dìngqī jiù shì sǐqī zhànghù.
Dà Wèi:	Wǒ xiān kāi yí ge huóqī zhànghù, guò jǐ tiān zài lái kāi yí ge dìngqī zhànghù.
Zhíyuán:	Hǎo! Qǐng tián yíxià zhè zhāng biǎo, bǎ dìzhǐ hé liánxì diànhuà xiě qīngchu.
Dà Wèi:	Lìngwài, wǒ xiǎng wèn yíxià, wàiguórén kěyǐ shēnqǐng xìnyòngkǎ ma?
Zhíyuán:	Bùguǎn shì wàiguórén háishi Zhōngguórén, dōu kěyǐ zài zhèli shēnqǐng xìnyòngkǎ. Wǒmen yǒu Chángchéng Rénmínbì xìnyòngkǎ hé Chángchéng guójì xìnyòngkǎ.
Dà Wèi:	Guójì xìnyòngkǎ yǐ shénme huòbì jiésuàn?
Zhíyuán:	Měiyuán hé Gǎngbì liǎng zhǒng.
Dà Wèi:	Wǒ shēnqǐng yí ge yǐ Měiyuán jiésuàn de Chángchéng guójì xìnyòngkǎ.
Zhíyuán:	Hǎo! Qǐng nǐ zài tián yì zhāng biǎo, qǐng hǎohǎo kàn yíxià shuōmíng zài tián.

Dialogue Two

Xiǎo Fāng:	Nǐ hǎo, wǒ de xìnyòngkǎ diū le.
Zhíyuán:	Nǐ de kǎhào shì duōshao?
Xiǎo Fāng:	00359486721.
Zhíyuán:	Xìngmíng?
Xiǎo Fāng:	Fāng Yīng.
Zhíyuán:	Dìzhǐ?
Xiǎo Fāng:	Xiānggǎng Lù 25 hào, 9 hào lóu 2 dānyuán 1 hào.
Zhíyuán:	Nǐ de xìnyòngkǎ mìmǎ shì duōshao?
Xiǎo Fāng:	Wǒ jì bu qīng le, hǎoxiàng shì "1225".
Zhíyuán:	Bú shì shùzì.
Xiǎo Fāng:	Xiǎng qǐlái le, shì "Nánjīng".
Zhíyuán:	Duì le. nǐ zuìhòu yí cì shǐyòng xìnyòngkǎ shì zài shénme shíhou, shénme dìfang?
Xiǎo Fāng:	Jīntiān zhōngwǔ, zài chāoshì. Wǒ mǎile liùshí duō kuài qián de dōngxi.
Zhíyuán:	Qǐng fàngxīn, nǐ de kǎ méi bèi dàoyòng.
Xiǎo Fāng:	Xiètiān xièdì!
Zhíyuán:	Nǐ de jiù kǎ yǐ bèi tíng yòng, xīn kǎ hěn kuài jiù huì jìdào nǐ de zhùchù.
Xiǎo Fāng:	Xièxie nǐ de bāngzhù.

Text

Zhōngguó Yínháng Xìnyòngkǎ

Zhōngguó Yínháng shì Zhōngguó zuì zhòngyào de yínháng zhī yī. 2005 nián Zhōngguó Yínháng zài Yīngguó "Yínháng Jiā" zázhì píngxuǎn chū de "Shìjiè 1000 jiā dà yínháng" zhōng míngliè dì 18 wèi.

Zhōngguó Yínháng de Chángchéng xìnyòngkǎ xìliè shēn shòu rénmen de xǐ'ài. Chángchéng xìnyòngkǎ pǐnzhǒng bāokuò Chángchéng diànzǐ jièjìkǎ, Chángchéng Rénmínbì xìnyòngkǎ pǔtōngkǎ, Chángchéng Rénmínbì xìnyòngkǎ zhàopiàn jīnkǎ, Chángchéng Rénmínbì xìnyòngkǎ jīnkǎ, Chángchéng guójì xìnyòngkǎ pǔtōngkǎ hé Chángchéng guójì xìnyòngkǎ jīnkǎ.

Zài Zhōngguó shēnqǐng xìnyòngkǎ, chúle yào yǒu gōngzuò yǐwài, nǐ de zhànghù li hái yào yǒu xiànjīn. Shēnqǐng Chángchéng Rénmínbì xìnyòngkǎ pǔtōngkǎ shí, nǐ de zhànghù li zuì shǎo dé yǒu 1000 yuán Rénmínbì. Nǐ kěyǐ zuì gāo tòuzhī 5000 yuán. Tòuzhī qī, yě jiù shì xìnyòng qī, wéi 60 tiān. Nǐ kěyǐ zài biāoyǒu Zhōngguó Yínháng Chángchéng xìnyòngkǎ biaojì de shāngdiàn, fàndiàn, jiǔlóu, jīchǎng, yīyuàn děng chǎngsuǒ, shǐyòng Chángchéng xìnyòngkǎ jié zhàng. Shǐyòng Chángchéng xìnyòngkǎ měi nián xū jiāonà 20 yuán de shǒuxùfèi.

Lesson 34   In a post office

Dialogue One

Xuésheng:	Nǐ hǎo! Wǒ jì yí ge bāoguǒ.
Zhíyuán:	Lǐmiàn shì shénme dōngxi?
Xuésheng:	Yí jiàn xiùhuā shuìyī, yí ge xiùhuā bèitào hé yì tiáo chuángdān.
Zhíyuán:	Ànzhào guīdìng, wǒ bìxū dǎkāi jiǎnchá yíxià.
Xuésheng:	Jiǎnchá ba, méi wèntí.
Zhíyuán:	Kànlái nǐ hěn xǐhuan Zhōngguó de shǒugōng xiùhuā zhìpǐn.
Xuésheng:	Bú shì wǒ, shì wǒ yéye nǎinai xǐhuan. Tāmen yídìng yào wǒ mǎi yìxiē jì huíqù.
Zhíyuán:	Nǐ jì nǎr?
Xuésheng:	Mǎdélǐ.
Zhíyuán:	Shì hǎiyùn háishi kōngyùn?
Xuésheng:	Kōngyùn. Wǒ xiǎng ràng tāmen zǎo diǎn shōudào.
Zhíyuán:	Hǎo! Chēng yíxià ba.
Xuésheng:	Duì le, wǒ hái xiǎng mǎi jǐ zhāng jìniàn yóupiào.
Zhíyuán:	Jīnnián shì zhū nián, wǒmen yǒu zhū nián jìniàn yóupiào.
Xuésheng:	Tài hǎo le! Wǒ shì shǔ zhū de, wǒ mǎi shí tào.

Dialogue Two

Xiǎo Wáng:	Xiǎo Lǐ, zhū nián de jìniàn yóupiào chūlai le, nǐ kàn, piàoliang ba?!
Xiǎo Lǐ:	Zhēn piàoliang!
Xiǎo Wáng:	Nǐ bú shì yě shǔ zhū ma? Kuài qù yóujú mǎi yí tào ba!
Xiǎo Lǐ:	Wǒ bù shǔ zhū, wǒ shǔ gǒu.
Xiǎo Wáng:	Zěnme huì ne?! Wǒmen dōu shì 1983 nián chūshēng de.
Xiǎo Lǐ:	Kě wǒ de shēngri shì yánglì 1 yuè, nà shí yīnlì háishi 1982 nián 12 yuè ne.
Xiǎo Wáng:	Yīnlì hé yánglì shì zěnme huí shì? Wǒ bú tài dǒng.
Xiǎo Lǐ:	Yánglì shì Xīfāngrén shǐyòng de lìfǎ, yīnlì shì Zhōngguórén shǐyòng de lìfǎ.
Xiǎo Wáng:	Wèishénme huì yǒu liǎng zhǒng bùtóng de lìfǎ?
Xiǎo Lǐ:	Yīnwèi wǒmen shì yǐ tàiyáng lái jìsuàn rìqī de, ér Zhōngguórén shì yǐ yuèliang lái jìsuàn de.
Xiǎo Wáng:	Wǒ míngbai le. Nà yīnlì hé yánglì xiāngchà jǐ tiān?
Xiǎo Lǐ:	Yí ge duō yuè.
Xiǎo Wáng:	Suǒyǐ yī yuèfèn chūshēng de rén bù yídìng shǔ dāngnián de shǔxiàng.
Xiǎo Lǐ:	Bù jǐnjǐn shì yī yuèfèn, èr yuè chū chūshēng de rén yě bù yídìng, bǐrú shuō Xiǎo Fāng.
Xiǎo Wáng:	Guàibudé Xiǎo Fāng de chuángtóu shang guàzhe yì zhī xiǎo gǒu, yuánlái tā yě shì shǔ gǒu de.

Text

Zěnyàng Zài Zhōngguó Jì Yóujiàn

Rúguǒ nǐ qù yóujú jì yóujiàn, yóujú de zhíyuán huì wèn nǐ shì jì hángkōng yóujiàn, shuǐ-lù-lù yóujiàn háishi kōngyùn shuǐ lù-lù yóujiàn. Dàodǐ nǎ yì zhǒng fāngfǎ hǎo ne?

Yīnggāi shuō gè yǒu gè de hǎochù. Hángkōng yóujiàn shíjiān kuài, yìbān yí ge xīngqī zuǒyòu jiù kěyǐ shōudào, suǒyǐ suīrán yóufèi jiào guì, hěn duō yònghù háishi xǐhuan shǐyòng zhè zhǒng yóujì fāngshì. Shuǐ-lù-lù yóujiàn shì shǐyòng qìchē, huǒchē huò lúnchuán lái yùnshū de, shíjiān bǐjiào cháng, kěshì yóufèi bǐjiào piányi. Kōngyùn shuǐ-lù-lù yóujiàn shì shǐyòng guójì hángbān, qìchē, huǒchē huò lúnchuán lái yóujì de. Shíjiān shang bǐ hángkōng yóujiàn màn, bǐ shuǐ lù-lù yóujiàn kuài; yóufèi shang bǐ hángkōng yóujiàn piányi, bǐ shuǐ-lù-lù yóujiàn guì, shì yònghù cháng yòng de yóujì fāngshì.

Yóujú li de fúwùyuán hái huì wèn nǐ shì jì píngcháng yóujiàn, guàhào yóujiàn háishi bǎojià yóujiàn. Jì píngcháng yóujiàn jì diūle yě méiyǒu bànfǎ cháxún, suǒyǐ rúguǒ shì guìzhòng de yóujiàn, yídìng yào jì guàhào. Rúguǒ nǐ jì de shì bāoguǒ, nà shì kěyǐ cháxún de. Dànshì rúguǒ nǐ méiyǒu bǎojià, diūshīle háishi dé bu dào péicháng, yīncǐ nǐ zuì hǎo jì bǎojià.

Lesson 35   At a barber's

Dialogue One

Xiǎo Fāng: Xiǎo Wáng, nǐ qù nǎr le? Wǒ dàochù zhǎo nǐ.

Xiǎo Wáng: Wǒ qù yóujú le, nǐ zhǎo wǒ yǒu shì ma?

Xiǎo Fāng: Nǐ de fàxíng búcuò, wǒ xiǎng wènwen nǐ shì zài nǎ jiā lǐfàdiàn lǐ de.

Xiǎo Wáng: Wǒ shì zài shìzhōngxīn de yì jiā lǐfàdiàn lǐ de.

Xiǎo Fāng: Nà jiā diàn jiào shénme míngzi?

Xiǎo Wáng: Xīnxīn Fàláng.

Xiǎo Fāng: Guì bu guì?

Xiǎo Wáng: Bú guì, liánjiǎn dàichuī yígòng cái sānshí kuài.

Xiǎo Fāng: Nàli yǒu méiyǒu nǚshì měifàbù?

Xiǎo Wáng: Yǒu, nàli bùjǐn lǐfà hé jiǎnfà, érqiě hái tàngfà hé rǎnfà.

Xiǎo Fāng: Tài hǎo le! Wǒ nǚpéngyou yào rǎnfà, wǒmen kěyǐ yìqǐ qù le.

Xiǎo Wáng: Zhè jiā lǐfàdiàn hěn máng, nǐ zuì hǎo zǎo diǎnr qù.

Xiǎo Fāng: Lǐfàdiàn jǐ diǎn kāi mén?

Xiǎo Wáng: Bā diǎn.

Xiǎo Fāng: Nǐ yǒu zhè jiā lǐfàdiàn de dìzhǐ ma?

Xiǎo Wáng: Méi yǒu, lǐfàdiàn jiù zài Dōngdān, nǐ xià chē hòu dǎting yíxià jiù zhīdào le.

Dialogue Two

Lǐfàyuán:	Nǐmen hǎo, qǐngjìn.
Xiǎo Fāng:	Nǐ hǎo. Ā, zhème duō rén pái duì!
Lǐfàyuán:	Wǒmen zhèr yǒu shí jǐ wèi shīfu, yíhuìr jiù lúndào nǐ le. Qǐng zuò.
Xiǎo Fāng:	Xièxie. Wǒmen xūyào ná yí ge hào ma?
Lǐfàyuán:	Wǒ lái bāng nǐ ná. Zhè wèi xiǎojiě yě shì lái měifà de ma?
Xiǎo Lǐ:	Duì, wǒ xiǎng bǎ tóufa rǎnchéng hēisè de.
Lǐfàyuán:	Hǎo. Búguò nǐ de jīnfà hěn piàoliang, rǎnchéng hēisè zhēn kěxī.
Xiǎo Lǐ:	Wǒ de jīnfà zài zhèr tài xiǎnyǎn le. Wǒ bù xiǎng yǐnqǐ rénmen de zhùyì.
Xiǎo Fāng:	Wǒ xiǎng lǐ yí ge duǎnfà, kě wǒ bù zhīdào nà jiào shénme fàxíng.
Lǐfàyuán:	Nà jiào bǎncùn, yě jiù shì píngtóu. Nǐ lǐ bǎncùn yídìng hěn shuài.
Xiǎo Lǐ:	Wǒ zǎo jiù xiǎng ràng tā huàn ge fàxíng, duǎnfà kàn qǐlái hěn jīngshen.
Xiǎo Fāng:	Xǐ qǐlái yě fāngbiàn.
Lǐfàyuán:	Méi cuòr. Yòu jīngshen yòu fāngbiàn, érqiě hěn shìhé nǐ de liǎnxíng.

Text

Běijīng de Lǐfàdiàn

Běijīng Shì hěn dà, yǒu jǐ bǎi ge lǐfàdiàn, yǒumíng de lǐfàdiàn yě yǒu jǐshí ge. Wángfǔjǐng Dàjiē de Měibái Měifàtīng jiù shì yǒumíng de lǐfàdiàn zhī yī. Gāi diàn kāiyè yú 1928 nián, shì Běijīng de yì jiā lǎozìhào, dāngshí jiào Měibái Lǐfàguǎn. Yīnwèi měiróng yǐjīng chéngwéi Měi- bái zhǔyào de yèwù, suǒyǐ xiànzài gǎi míng wéi Měibái Lǐfàtīng. Měibái yǒu hěn duō chūsè de Lǐfàshī hé měiróngshī, jǐn tèjí lǐfàshī jiù yǒu sān rén.

Sìlián měifà měiróng gōngsī yě wèi yú Wángfǔjǐng Dàjiē shang, shì "2000 nián Zhōngguó zuì hǎo de měifà měiróng yuàn" zhī yī. Sìlián shè yǒu "nǚbīn lǐfà", "nánbīn lǐfà", "měiróngshì", nánbīn měifà "guìbīntīng" hé nǚbīn měifà "míngrénshì".

Běijīngrén zuì ài bǎncùn, zhè zhǒng fàxíng lǎo-zhōng-qīng dōu shìhé. Lǐ bǎncùn měi rén cái 30 yuán, yòu piányi yòu hǎokàn. Běijīng de Jīnbǎncùn Lǐfàdiàn zhuān lǐ bǎncùn, fēicháng yǒumíng. Zhōngguó hěn duō hángtiānyuán dōu shì nàli de gùkè.

Lesson 36   Asking for leave

Dialogue One

Xiǎo Wáng:	Xiǎo Lǐ, kuài qǐchuáng, shàng kè yào chídào le!
Xiǎo Lǐ:	Wǒ jīntiān bù shūfu, bùnéng qù shàngkè le.
Xiǎo Wáng:	Nǐ zěnme la? Nǎr bù shūfu?
Xiǎo Lǐ:	Wǒ zuówǎn chīle xiē kǎoyángròu, méi xiǎngdào lāqǐ dùzi lái le.
Xiǎo Wáng:	Shì bu shì yángròu bù xīnxiān le?
Xiǎo Lǐ:	Shuí zhīdào ne! Yě kěnéng shì méiyǒu kǎoshú.
Xiǎo Wáng:	Yào bu yào qù yīyuàn kànkan?
Xiǎo Lǐ:	Bú yòng le, wǒ yǐjīng chīle yào.
Xiǎo Wáng:	Nà nǐ hǎohāo xiūxi, wǒ bāng nǐ qǐngjià.
Xiǎo Lǐ:	Wǒ gěi lǎoshī xiě ge qǐngjiàtiáo ba.
Xiǎo Wáng:	Nǐ néng xiě ma? Yào bu yào wǒ tì nǐ xiě?
Xiǎo Lǐ:	Bú yòng, wǒ zìjǐ néng xiě. Āi, nǐ zhīdào zěnme yòng Zhōngwén xiě qǐngjiàtiáo ma?
Xiǎo Wáng:	Shū shang yǒu xiànchéng de lìzi, chāo yí ge qiānshàng zìjǐ de míngzi jiù xíng le.
Xiǎo Lǐ:	Nà zěnme xíng! Qǐngjià de yuányīn bù kěnéng xiāngtóng a!
Xiǎo Wáng:	Nǐ zhēn bèn, nǐ bǎ tóuténg gǎichéng lādùzi jiù xíng le.
Xiǎo Lǐ:	Zhè shì ge hǎo fāngfǎ! Háishi nǐ cōngmíng.

Dialogue Two

Xiǎo Wáng:	Xiǎo Lǐ, nǐ zài xiě shénme?
Xiǎo Lǐ:	Wǒ zài xiě tōngzhī.
Xiǎo Wáng:	Shì guānyú shénme de tōngzhī?
Xiǎo Lǐ:	Yīnyuè jiǎngzuò de.
Xiǎo Wáng:	Nǐ zhīdào tōngzhī hé tōnggào yǒu shénme bùtóng ma?
Xiǎo Lǐ:	Dōu chàbuduō, búguò tōnggào bǐ tōngzhī gèngjiā zhèngshì yìdiǎnr.
Xiǎo Wáng:	Tōnggào shì bu shì bǐ tōngzhī gèng dà yìdiǎnr?
Xiǎo Lǐ:	Jiù fànwéi éryán, duì. Yīnwèi tōngzhī dàduō shì duì nèi de, tōnggào shì duì wài de.
Xiǎo Wáng:	Guàibudé wǒ jīngcháng tīng rén shuō zhè shì nèibù tōngzhī, bù gōngkāi.
Xiǎo Lǐ:	Méi cuòr.
Xiǎo Wáng:	Kěyǐ shuō tōnggào jiù shì gōngkāi de tōngzhī ma?
Xiǎo Lǐ:	Kěyǐ zhème shuō.
Xiǎo Wáng:	Āi, nǐ hái zhīdào tōnggào hé guǎnggào de qūbié ma?
Xiǎo Lǐ:	Guǎnggào jiù shì guǎngérgàozhī de yìsi, shì wèi shāngyè fúwù de. Diànshì shang tiāntiān dōu yǒu.
Xiǎo Wáng:	Nà gōnggào ne?
Xiǎo Lǐ:	Jiù shì gōngkāi gàosu nǐ ya!

Text

Zěnyàng Xiě Qǐngjià Tiáo hé Tōngzhī

Dāng nǐ yǒu jǐ shì bùnéng qù shàngbān huòzhě shàngkè shí, nǐ xūyào xiě zhāng qǐnjià tiáo qǐngjià. Xiě qǐngjiàtiáo yìbān bù xiě dìzhǐ, dàn bìxū xiě qīngchu shōu jiàtiáo de rén shì shuí, qǐngjià de rén shì shuí, qǐngjià de yuányīn, qǐngjià duōcháng shíjiān hé xiě qǐngjiàtiáo de shíjiān.

Rúguǒ nǐ yǒu huódòng xūyào shìxiān gàosu cānjiā de rényuán, nǐ kěyǐ yòng liǎng zhǒng fāngshì tōngzhī. Yì zhǒng fāngshì shì kǒutóu gàosu tāmen, zhè jiàozuò kǒutóu tōngzhī. Lìng yì zhǒng fāngshì shì yòng wénzì gàosu tāmen, zhè jiào zuò shūmiàn tōngzhī. Xiě shūmiàn tōngzhī yào xiě qīngchu shíjiān, dìdiǎn, shìqíng hé cānjiā rényuán, zuì hòu yào xiě shàng fā tōngzhī de dānwèi hé rìqī. Nǐ hái kěyǐ zài tōngzhī qiánmiàn jiā shàng "zhòngyào", "jǐnjí" děng zìyàng, yǐ yǐnqǐ rénmen de zhùyì. Qǐng kàn xiàlì.

Qǐngjià Tiáo

Zūnjìng de Huáng lǎoshī:

Jīntiān wǒ bìng le, lā dùzi, bù néng qù shàngkè le, fēicháng bàoqiàn. Qǐngqiú lǎoshī zhǔn jiǎ yì tiān.

cǐzhì

Jìnglǐ

Nǐ de xuésheng: Lǐ Guì

11 yuè 16 rì

Tōngzhī

Wǔ yuè sì rì Xīngqīsān xiàwǔ, shāngxuéyuàn de Yú Yuànzhǎng jiāng lái wǒ xiào zuò guānyú jiùyè wèntí de zhuāntí jiǎngzuò. Jiǎngzuò jiāng yú xiàwǔ liǎngdiǎn zhèngshì kāishǐ, qǐng tóngxuémen yú liǎngdiǎn yǐqián dào wǔ hào Lóu èr céng dà jiàoshì jiùzuò.

Xuéshēnghuì

4 yuè 22 rì

Lesson 37   Writing a letter

Dialogue One

Xiǎo Zhāng:	Xiǎo Lǐ, nǐ jì de xìn gěi tuì huílái le.
Xiǎo Lǐ:	Zěnme huí shì?
Xiǎo Zhāng:	Xìnfēng de géshì bú duì, nǐ bǎ dìzhǐ xiě fǎn le.
Xiǎo Lǐ:	Xiě fǎn le? Nándào shì jìxìnrén dìzhǐ zài xià, shōuxìnrén dìzhǐ zài shàng?
Xiǎo Zhāng:	Dāngrán la!
Xiǎo Lǐ:	Zěnme Zhōngguó zhèr shénme dōu shì xiāngfǎn de?!
Xiǎo Zhāng:	Nà bújiàndé.
Xiǎo Lǐ:	Nǐ kàn, Zhōngguó kāi chē kào yòu xíng, Yīngguó kāi chē kào zuǒ xíng.
Xiǎo Zhāng:	Dàbùfen guójiā dōu shì kào yòu xíng, zhǐ yǒu shǎoshù jǐ ge guójiā lìwài.
Xiǎo Lǐ:	Zhōngguórén xìng zài qián, míng zài hòu.
Xiǎo Zhāng:	Ālābó guójiā yě shì zhèyàng.
Xiǎo Lǐ:	Zhōngguórén biǎodá rìqī cóng dà dào xiǎo, Xīfāngrén shì cóng xiǎo dào dà.
Xiǎo Zhāng:	Rìběnrén jiù shì cóng dà dào xiǎo de.
Xiǎo Lǐ:	Zhōngguó nánrén chuān qúnzi, liú biànzi.
Xiǎo Zhāng:	Zhēn de, wǒ zěnme méi kànjiàn?! Nǐ shì zài nǎr kànjiàn de?
Xiǎo Lǐ:	Zài diànyǐng li.
Xiǎo Zhāng:	Wǒ shuō ne. Búguò nà bú shì qúnzi, nà shì páozi.
Xiǎo Lǐ:	Nà liú biànzi shì zěnme huíshì?
Xiǎo Zhāng:	Xiànzài bú shì yǒu hěn duō nánrén liú biànzi ma? Shìjiè shì duōyuán de.

Text

Qīn'ài de Gāo lǎoshī:

Nín hǎo! Shíjiān guò de zhēn kuài. Wǒmen lái Zhōngguó yǐjīng yí ge yuè le. Zhèlǐ de yíqiè dōu hěn hǎo, qǐng bú yào guàniàn. Wǒmen xiànzài měi zhōu shàng 18 ge xiǎoshí de kè. Wǒmen yǒu liù-qī mén kè. Wǒ hěn xǐhuan kǒuyǔkè hé yǔfǎkè, nǐ zhīdào wǒ de yǔyīn yǔdiào bú tài hǎo, yǔfǎ de cuòwù yě hěn duō, shàng zhè liǎng mén kè wǒ de shōuhuò hěn dà. Zhèlǐ de lǎoshī quánbù dōu yòng Hànyǔ jiǎngkè. Yì kāishǐ wǒ gǎndào fēicháng chīlì, xiànzài wǒ yǐjīng xíguàn le.

Wǒ xiànzài zhù zài xuéxiào de liúxuéshēng sùshè li, zhèlǐ de jūzhù tiáojiàn fēicháng hǎo, gēn dà fàndiàn chàbuduō. Fángjiān li yǒu diànshì hé kōngtiáo, měi tiān hái yǒu fúwùyuán lái dǎsǎo fángjiān. Wǒ dōu gěi guànhuài le. Xuéxiào de cāntīng yě hěn búcuò, búguò Běijīng de shíwù fēicháng piányi, wǒ chángcháng hé tóngxué chūqu chī fàn. Wǒ hěn xǐhuan chī kǎoyā hé Gǒubùlǐ bāozi.

Lái Běijīng qián nín gàosu wǒmen Běijīng yòu dà yòu piàoliang, kěshì wǒ méiyǒu xiǎng dào Běijīng yǒu zhème dà, zhème piàoliang! Fùshàng jǐ zhāng zhàopiàn, zhè shì wǒ hé Lǐ Jiàn zài xiàoyuán li pāi de. Wǒmen hái méiyǒu hǎohāo chūqu wánguo.

Zhōngguórén hěn hàokè, wǒ yǐjīng jiāole bù shǎo péngyou. Wǒ hái yǒu yí ge yǔyán huǒbàn, tā jiào Yú Àihuá, shì yīngyǔxì de xuésheng. Hěn duō rén wù yǐwéi tā shì wǒ nǚpéngyou. Búguò wǒ dào shì xīwàng rúcǐ, yīnwèi tā rén hěn hǎo, zhǎng de yòu fēicháng piàoliang. Guānyú tā, wǒ yǒu hěn duō yào duì nín shuō de, jīntiān jiù xiě dào zhèr ba. Wǒ hái yào zhǔnbèi míngtiān de tīngxiě ne.

Děngzhe nín de huíxìn.

Zhù nín shēntǐ jiànkāng!

Nín de xuésheng: Wáng Jīng

Lesson 38   Applying for a job

Dialogue One

Àihuá:	Xiǎo Wáng, nǐ bú shì yào zhǎo ge gōngsī shíxí ma? Nǐ kànkan zhè ge guǎnggào.
Xiǎo Wáng:	Zhāopìn shíxíshēng, měi zhōu gōngzuò liù xiǎoshí. Yǒuyì zhě qǐng jì jiǎnlì lái.
Àihuá:	Gōngzī hěn gāo, měi xiǎoshí wǔshí kuài.
Xiǎo Wáng:	Wǒ mǎshàng gēn tāmen liánxì.
Àihuá:	Nǐ xūyào yì fēng qiúzhí xìn hé yí fèn Zhōngwén jiǎnlì.
Xiǎo Wáng:	Wǒ zhèr yǒu yí fèn Zhōngwén jiǎnlì, nǐ bāng wǒ kànkan, hǎo bu hǎo?
Àihuá:	Hǎo... Xiǎo Wáng, méi xiǎngdào nǐ jūrán shì ge niúpí dàwáng!
Xiǎo Wáng:	Nǐ shuō shénme?! Wǒ nǎr chuī le?
Àihuá:	"Cáihuá chūzhòng, jīngtōng Hànyǔ děng wǔ guó yǔyán".
Xiǎo Wáng:	Zhè bú shì chuīniú, zhǐ shì yǒudiǎnr kuāzhāng.
Àihuá:	Bú shì yǒudiǎnr kuāzhāng, ér shì tài kuāzhāng le.
Xiǎo Wáng:	Bù kuāzhāng zěnme néng bǎ zìjǐ tuīxiāo chūqu?
Àihuá:	Zhōngguórén zuì bù xǐhuan zhè yàng de rén, Lǎo Wáng mài guā, zìmài zìkuā.
Xiǎo Wáng:	Wǒ shì xìng Wáng, kěshì wǒ méiyǒu mài guā.
Àihuá:	Hǎo, nǐ méi yǒu mài guā. Nǐ bú shì jīngtōng Hànyǔ ma? Zěnme lián zhè jù huà yě bù dǒng. Xué yǔyán bù xuéxí wénhuà shì bù xíng de.
Xiǎo Wáng:	Hǎo, shì wǒ cuò le, wǒ bù gāi chuīniú. Nǐ bāng wǒ gǎigai hǎo bu hǎo?
Àihuá:	Nǐ bú pà tuīxiāo bù chūqu le?
Xiǎo Wáng:	Bú pà. Yǐ nǐ de nénglì, wǒ de zīlì, tuīxiāo bù chūqu cái guài ne.
Àihuá:	Ā! Nǐ hái zài chuī a!

Text One

Qiúzhí Xìn

Zūnjìng de Zhōu Xiǎojiě,

Cóng bào shang wǒ kàndào guì háng zhèngzài zhāopìn shíxíshēng, wǒ duì cǐ gōngzuò shífēn gǎn xìngqù. Tè xiě cǐ xìn shēnqǐng.

Wǒ yìzhí duì yínhángyè shífēn gǎn xìngqù. Gāozhōng bìyè hòu wǒ jiù dào Huángjiā Sūgélán Yínháng shíxíle yì nián. Wǒ xiànzài shì Lúndūn Ōuzhōu Shāngxuéyuàn dà'èr de xuésheng, mùqián zài Běijīng Yǔyán Dàxué xuéxí Hànyǔ. Wǒ huì shuō duō zhǒng yǔyán, shúxī yínháng yèwù, tèbié shì xìnyòngkǎ yèwù. Wǒ wéirén rèqíng, lèyú zhùrén. Wǒ xiǎng wǒ yídìng néng shèngrèn zhè ge gōngzuò.

Fùshàng wǒ de jiǎnlì. Qǐng cháshōu.

Cǐzhì

Jìnglǐ

qiúzh rén: Wáng Jīng

2006 nián 5 yuè 16 rì

Text Two

Gèrén Jiǎnlì

Xìngmín: Wáng Jīng

Chūshēng niányuè: 1982 nián 2 yuè 7 rì

Guójí: Yīngguó

Liánxì dìzhǐ:　　Běijīng DōngchéngQū Jiànguó Lù 123 hào

Liánxì fāngshì: shǒujī diànhuà: 013987556398　chuánzhēn: 010 32986745

Diànzǐ xìnxiāng: daweiwang@yahoo.com.cn

Xuélì:

2001 nián 9 yuè — zhì jīn	Lúndūn Ōuzhōu Shāngxuéyuàn xuésheng
1994 nián 9 yuè — 2000 nián 7 yuè	Sūgélán Jīnshān Zhōngxué xuésheng
1988 nián 8 yuè — 1994 nián 7 yuè	Lúndūn Hǎidé Xiǎoxué xuésheng

Gōngzuò jīnglì:

2003 nián 9 yuè — zhì jīn	Yīngyǔ jiātíng jiàoshī
2000 nián 8 yuè — 2001 nián 8 yuè	Huángjiā Sūgélán Yínháng shíxíshēng
1998 nián 7 yuè — 1998 nián 9 yuè	Jīnshān jiànzhù gōngsī shíxíshēng

Gōngzuò xìngqù:　　Yínháng fēngxiǎn guǎnlǐ, xìnyòngkǎ yèwù, sīrén yínháng yèwù

Jìnéng:　　　　Jīngtōng jìsuànjī; huì shuō sì guó yǔyán — Yīngyǔ, Déyǔ, Yìdàlìyǔ, Hànyǔ

Àihào:　　　　Pá shān, qí mǎ, tiào wǔ, kǎlā-OK, shàng wǎng

Lesson 39   Shopping

Dialogue One

Wáng Jīng:	Xièxie nǐ péi wǒ shàngjiē gòuwù.
Àhuá:	Bú yòng xiè, wǒ zuì xǐhuan guàng shāngdiàn le.
Wáng Jīng:	Nà wǒmen jīntiān jiù hǎohāo guàngguang.
Àihuá:	Nǐ dōu dǎsuan mǎi shénme?
Wáng Jīng:	Suíbiàn guàngguang, kàndào shénme hǎo jiù mǎi shénme.
Àihuá:	Yágāo, yáshuā, xiāngzào, féizào nǐ dōu mǎi qí le ma?
Wáng Jīng:	Yǔqí shuō shì mǎi qí le, bùrú shuō shì dài qí le. Zhè xiē dōngxi wǒ dōu shì cóng Yīngguó dàilái de.
Àihuá:	Tiān a, yǒu zhège bìyào ma?!
Wáng Jīng:	Wǒ yòng guànle xīfāng de páizi, pà zài Zhōngguó mǎi bu dào.
Àihuá:	Wǒ dài nǐ qù bǎihuòdàlóu kànkan, nàli de xīfāng rìyòngpǐn duō de bùdéliǎo.
Wáng Jīng:	Nà kě tài hǎo le! Zǒu, wǒmen qù bǎihuò dàlóu.
Àihuá:	Běijīng de zìyóu shìchǎng yě búcuò.
Wáng Jīng:	Nàli de dōngxi duō ma?
Àihuá:	Duō! Nàli yào shénme yǒu shénme, érqiě wùměi jiàlián.
Wáng Jīng:	Nà wǒmen hái děng shénme, qù zìyóu shìchǎng!

Dialogue Two

Dàniáng:	Xiǎohuǒzi, nǐ xūyào mǎi yì tiáo xīn niúzǎikù le.
Wáng Jīng:	Dàniáng, nǐ gǎocuò le, wǒ kùzi shang de dòng shì gùyì nòngpò de.
Dàniáng:	Wǒ zhīdào, kěshì zhè yǐjīng bú shì zuì xīn kuǎnshì le.
Wáng Jīng:	Bú huì ba, wǒ lái zhīqián gāng mǎi de.
Dàniáng:	Wǒ bú huì piàn nǐ de, nǐ kàn, zhè cái shì xiànzài liúxíng de kuǎnshì.
Àihuá:	Zhè kuǎnshì búcuò, féiféi-dàdà de, lǐmiàn néng zhuāng yì tóu gǒuxióng.
Dàniáng:	Tiānqì lěng le, lǐmiàn jiā tiáo máokù zhèng hǎo.
Wáng Jīng:	Wǒ zhǐ chuān dānkù, cónglái méi chuānguo máokù.
Dàniáng:	Kànlái nǐ hái méi zài Běijīng guòguo dōng, Běijīng zhèr dōngtiān lěng de hěn.
Àihuá:	Yǒu nuǎnqì, méiguānxi.
Dàniáng:	Gūniang, nǐ yě mǎi tiáo chángqún ba, nǐ nà chāoduǎnqún guò bu liǎo dōng.
Àihuá:	Dàniáng, chángqún tài guì le, wǒ mǎi bu qǐ.
Dàniáng:	Qiáo nǐ shuō de, nǐ yǒu ge wàiguó nánpéngyou, zěnme huì mǎi bu qǐ?!
Wáng Jīng:	Dàniáng, tā hái bú shì wǒ de nǚpéngyou.
Dàniáng:	Nà jiù kuài zhuī! Lái, zhè tiáo liányīqún zuótiān gāng dào, tā chuān zhènghǎo.
Wáng Jīng:	Zhēn piàoliang! Wǒmen yào le.
Àihuá:	Bù xíng bu xíng, jiàgé tài guì le! Gěi ge yōuhuì jià ba?

Dàniáng:　　　Hǎo, wǒ dǎ bā zhé mài gěi nǐmen, shuí jiào wǒ yí jiàndào nǐmen jiù xǐhuan ne!

Wáng Jīng:　　Xièxie dàniáng.

Text

"Dōngxi "Zhè Dōngxi Zhēn Shì ge Guài "Dōngxi"

　　Xuéxí "dōngxi" nà yí kè shí, wǒ zǒushén le. Hòulái lǎoshī wèn wǒ zhīdào bù zhīdào zěnme yòng "dōngxi" yì cí. Wǒ shuō: "Dāngrán zhīdào. Wǒmen kěyǐ shuō zhuōzi shì 'dōngxī', kěshì bù néng shuō 'Nǐ shì dōngxi' huòzhě 'Wǒ shì dōngxi', yīnwèi wǒmen dōu bú shì 'dōngxi'." Lǎoshī yì tīng jí le, máng shuō: "Bú duì, bú duì, bù néng shuō 'Wǒ bú shì dōngxi'." Wǒ liánmáng shuō: "Ā, duìbuqǐ, nǐ shì dōngxi." Lǎoshī shuō: "Yě bù néng shuō 'Nǐ shì dōngxi'." Wǒ yì tīng yě jí le "Nà nǐ dàodǐ shì shénme dōngxī?" Lǎoshī dāngchǎng qì de bàn sǐ, tóngxuémen lè de sǐqù-huólái.

　　Xiànzài wǒ zhīdàole "Nǐ bú shì dōngxi" shì mà rén de huà, "Nǐ shì shénme dōngxi" yě shì mà rén de huà. "Dōngxi" zhè dōngxi zhēn shì ge guài "dōngxi", shǐyòng "dōngxi" zhè ge cí shí kě děi qiānwàn xiǎoxīn na.

Lesson 40　Palace Museum

Dialogue One

Xiǎo Wáng:　　　Tóngzhì, wǒ mǎi yì zhāng Gùgōng Bówùguǎn de ménpiào.

Shòupiàoyuán:　Liùshí kuài yì zhāng.

Xiǎo Wáng:　　　Tīngshuō xuésheng yōuhuì, zhè shì wǒ de xuéshēngzhèng.

Shòupiàoyuán:　Duì, xuésheng èrshí kuài yì zhāng.

Xiǎo Wáng:　　　Wǒ hái xiǎng cānguān Tiān'ānmén hé Rénmín Dàhuìtáng, nǐmen mài bu mài tōngpiào?

Shòupiàoyuán:　Duìbuqǐ, wǒmen xiànzài hái méiyǒu zhè ge yèwù.

Xiǎo Wáng:　　　Rénmín Dàhuìtáng jīntiān hǎoxiàng tíngzhǐ cānguān, nǐ zhīdào wèishénme ma?

Shòupiàoyuán:　Jīntiān yǒu zhòngyào wàibīn láifǎng, Zǒnglǐ yào zài nàr jǔxíng huānyíng yànhuì.

Xiǎo Wáng:　　　Nà wǒ hái kěyǐ cānguān Máo Zhǔxí Jìniàntáng ma?

Shòupiàoyuán:　Kěyǐ, búguò děi děngdào huānyíng yíshì jiéshù zhī hòu.

Xiǎo Wáng:　　　Wǒ xiān cānguān Gùgōng, yí ge xiǎoshí hòu chūlái zhènghǎo.

Shòupiàoyuán:　Gùgōng hěn dà, méiyǒu liǎng-sān ge xiǎoshí nǐ chū bu lái.

Xiǎo Wáng:　　　Shì ma? Nà wǒ děi gǎnkuài jìnqù. Xièxie.

Shòupiàoyuán:　Búkèqi.

Dialogue Two

Xiǎo Wáng:	Qǐng wèn, cānguān Máo Zhǔxí Jìniàntáng shì zài zhèr pái duì ma?
Xiǎo Lǐ:	Shì de, búguò nǐ děi xiān qù cún bāo.
Xiǎo Wáng:	Wǒ de bāo li méi shénme dōngxi.
Xiǎo Lǐ:	Cānguān Jìniàntáng bù zhǔn dài rènhé dōngxi.
Xiǎo Wáng:	Zhàoxiàngjī yě bù néng dài ma?
Xiǎo Lǐ:	Bù néng dài. Lǐmiàn jìnzhǐ zhào xiàng.
Xiǎo Wáng:	Qǐng wèn cúnbāochù zài nǎr?
Xiǎo Lǐ:	Zài dōngmiànr. Nǐ kàn, hǎo duō rén zài nàr pái duì.
Xiǎo Wáng:	Zhème cháng de duì! Wǒ bù yīnggāi jīntiān lái.
Xiǎo Lǐ:	Tiāntiān dōu shì zhèyàng.
Xiǎo Wáng:	Zhōngguórén zhēn duō.
Xiǎo Lǐ:	Běijīng shì zhòngyào de lǚyóu jǐngdiǎn, rén géwài duō.

Text

Gùgōng

Gùgōng Bówùguǎn wèi yú Běijīng shìzhōngxīn, shì Míng, Qīng liǎng dài de huánggōng, xiānhòu jūzhùguo 24 wèi huángdì. Míng Qīng shí chēng wéi Zǐjìnchéng, 1925 nián kāishǐ chēng wéi Gùgōng. Gùgōng Bówùguǎn zhàndì qīshí'èr wàn duō píngfāngmǐ, yǒu fángwū jiǔqiān duō jiān, shì dāngjīn shìjiè shang xiàncún guīmó zuì dà, bǎocún zuì wánhǎo de gǔdài huánggōng jiànzhùqún.

Zhè zuò gùgōng wèishénme chēng wéi Zǐjìnchéng ne? Yuánlái, Zhōngguó gǔdài tiānwénxuéjiā rènwéi Zǐwēi Xīng jū yú zhōngtiān, shì Tiāndì suǒ zài. Yīn'ér, bǎ Tiāndì suǒ jūzhù de tiāngōng jiàozuò Zǐgōng. Huángdì zì chēng shì Tiāndì de érzi, shì zhēnlóng tiānzǐ, yīn'ér tāmen suǒ jūzhù de huánggōng yě bèi chēng wéi Zǐgōng. Huánggōng shì jìndì, shì bù néng suíbiàn chūrù de, suǒyǐ yòu bèi chēng wéi Zǐjìnchéng.

附录四　Appendix 4

练习答案　Keys to the Exercises

预备课

听力练习－Listening Practice

1.a　2.c　3.c　4.a　5.b　6.c　7.c　8.b

语法练习－Grammar Practice

单项选择

1.b　2.c　3.c　4.a　5.b　6.c　7.b　8.a　9.c　10.a

选词填空

着、着、正、着、正、正、得、到、就、得、了、过

认字识词－Words with Known Characters

名词	noun	动词	verb
形容词	adjective	副词	adverb
代词	pronoun	专有名词	proper noun
数词	numeral	量词	measure word
介词	preposition	连词	conjunction
感叹词	interjection	象声词	onomatopoeia

翻译练习－Translation

1. 我能把行李放（在）这儿吗？

2. 书太多了，我的包装不下。

3. 去德比的票多少钱一张？

4. 你能先帮我付上酒钱吗？

5. 交通是这儿最大的问题。

6. 上海的天气和伦敦的差不多。

7. 你的行李太重了，你不能把它带上飞机。

8. 我十二月总是很忙，忙到连去看我妈妈的时间都没有。

9. 我没想到他已经六十多岁了，因为他看起来只有四十几/多岁。

10. 对不起，我得先看看你的护照才可以给你票。

Lesson 31

听力练习－ Listening Practice

1.c   2.a   3.b   4.c   5.b   6.a   7.b   8.c

语法练习－ Grammar Practice

单项选择

1.b   2.c   3.a   4.a   5.c   6.b   7.a   8.c

选词填空

读、考试、一起、如果、可以、报到、和、然后、到、参加

认字识词－ Words with Known Characters

1.

总数	total amount	注意	pay attention to/attention
画册	pictorial	杂物	miscellaneous goods
思想	thinking/ideology	游览	tour/sightseeing
阅读	reading	比如	for instance
修理	repair	学科	subject of study

2.

老汉	old man	老虎	tiger
老公	husband	老婆	wife
老大	eldest child	老小	youngest child
小吃	snack	小费	tip
小店	little shop	小菜	common dish; side dish
小人书	picture story book	小朋友	children

翻译练习－ Translation

1. 大英图书馆的阅览室没有空调。

2. 我们明天十二点在我办公室对面的咖啡馆见面，好吗？

3. 我找不到你的名字。你订房间了吗？

4. 要学习中文/汉语的同学请到二楼注册。

5. 我是从越南来的，他是从马里来的。

6. 你得先付房钱，不然我不能给你钥匙。

Lesson 32

听力练习－ Listening Practice

1.c   2.c   3.a   4.a   5.b   6.c   7.a   8.c   9.c   10.b

语法练习－ Grammar Practice

单项选择

1.b   2.c   3.a   4.b   5.a   6.c   7.a   8.b

选词填空

那儿、种、爱好者、感觉、差不多、一开始、就像、平地

认字识词－ Words with Known Characters

1.	选美	pageant	干活	work
	私自	secretively	自私	selfish
	武打	gongfu fight	目前	for the time being
	活鱼	live fish	死人	deceased
	队长	team leader	证人	witness
2.	男子	man	演员	actor/actress
	脑子	brain	卫生员	health worker
	篮子	basket	警卫员	guard
	读者	reader	科学家	scientist
	记者	journalist	歌唱家	singer
	作者	writer	数学家	mathmatician

翻译练习－ Translation

1. 他昨天又迟到了，可是他好像一点儿也不觉得不好意思。

2. 我女朋友现在不仅每天去健身房，而且还请了一个私人教练。

3. 乒乓球在中国很流行，大部分大学都有球队。

4. 他不是不想吃，而是病了吃不下。

5. 中国书法很漂亮，可是看起来很难学。你觉得我学得会吗？

6. 我们什么时候可以注册功夫课？我从小就对功夫很感兴趣。

Lesson 33

听力练习－ Listening Practice

1.a   2.c   3.c   4.b   5.b   6.a   7.a   8.b

语法练习－ Grammar Practice

单项选择

1.c   2.b   3.a   4.a   5.b   6.a   7.c   8.b

选词填空

了、过、多少、当时、最高的、站着、先进、进口

认字识词－ Words with Known Characters

1.	管理	manage	管家	housekeeper
	账本	(account) book	算账	settle account, pay bill
	奖金	bonus	丢面子	lose face
	提货单	bill of landing/delivery order	寄存处	(luggage) deposit, left luggage
	香水	perfume	香米	fragrant rice
2.	道路	road	喜爱	love
	数量	amount	变化	change
	歌唱	sing	城市	city
	光亮	light	生产	produce
	表格	form	等候	wait
	偷盗	steal	存放	deposit, leave with

翻译练习－ Translation

1. 不管他去不去，我们明天都要去。

2. 谢天谢地，我的钱包没丢。我差点把我的信用卡停了。

3. 现在信用卡都要有个人密码。

4. 如果你想申请这个工作，你得填张表寄给这个公司。

5. 香港人很多，房子一般都很高，但是房间都比较小。

6. 用自动取款机取钱很方便，你什么时候取都行。

Lesson 34

听力练习－ Listening Practice

1.c　　2.b　　3.c　　4.a　　5.a　　6.c　　7.b　　8.a　　9.b　　10.a

语法练习－ Grammar Practice

单项选择

1.a　　2.c　　3.a　　4.c　　5.b　　6.a　　7.b　　8.a

选词填空

一般、又、使用、中间、到、小月、如、只有

认字识词－ Words with Known Characters

1.	按时	on time, on schedule	准时	on time, punctual
	念书	study/read	价格	price
	阳光	sunshine	月光	Moon light
	邮电局	post office	警察局	police station
	问询处	Information desk	办事处	office
2.	始终	from beginning to end	长短	length
	阴阳	Yin and Yang	是非	right and wrong
	老少	old and young	冷热	cold and hot; temperature
	真假	true and falsc	死活	life or death; anyway
	来往	contact	文武	civil and military
	早晚	sooner or later	轻重	weight

翻译练习－ Translation

1. 按照规定，你不应该把肉制品带进这个国家。

2. 我想买一些北京的纪念邮票。

3. 我是1985年出生的，你知道我属什么吗？

4. 我原来（是）吃肉（的），后来医生告诉我最好多吃蔬菜和水果。从那以后，我就再也不吃肉了/我就再也没吃过肉。

5. 为什么我上个月在中国寄的包裹还没有到？

6. 你的包裹是怎么寄的？海运还是空运？

Lesson 35

听力练习－ Listening Practice

1.b   2.c   3.a   4.b   5.c   6.b   7.c   8. a

语法练习－ Grammar Practice

单项选择

1.b   2.a   3.b   4.c   5.c   6.b   7.a   8.c

选词填空

让、再、顾客、按照、还是、虽然、起来、可以、而是、正在

认字识词－ Words with Known Characters

1.	护士	nurse	走廊	corridor
	明显	obvious	英寸	inch
	洗钱	money laundering	照顾	look after
	洗礼	baptize	宾馆	guest house
	染色体	chromosome	井井有条	in perfect order
2.	黑板	blackboard	明文	proclaimed in writing
	红牌	red card	黄牌	yellow card
	美酒	fine wine	香菜	coriander
	怪话	cynical remarks	短路	short circuit

平地	flat land	冷盘	cold dish
空位	empty seat	旧车	old car

翻译练习－ Translation

1. 我喜欢短头发，洗起来很容易/很容易洗。

2. 那儿烫发和染发都很便宜，连烫带染不到50英镑。

3. 他看起来有点生气了。我知道他已经一个多月没有休息了。

4. 伦敦位于英国的东南部，离海不远。

5. 王先生是位特级理发师，头发理得好极了。

6. 排队的人很多，要两个小时才能轮到你。

Lesson 36

听力练习－ Listening Practice

1.c   2.a   3.b   4.b   5.a   6.a   7.c   8.b

语法练习－ Grammar Practice

单项选择

1.c   2.b   3.a   4.b   5.b   6.a   7.c   8.a

选词填空

关于、本来、范围、以为、出去、正式、容易、只好、不管、非常

认字识词－ Words with Known Characters

1.	办法	method	同事	colleague
	内科	internal medicine	外科	surgery
	笨蛋	fool	地区	region
	签证	visa	拉面	hand-made noodles
	笨头笨脑	blunder head	笨手笨脚	clumsy
2.	倒茶	pour tea	洗车	wash car
	经商	do business	扫地	sweep floor
	越级	bypass the line manager	种菜	grow/plant vegetables

打字	typing	放羊	herding sheep
打鱼	fishing	生孩子	give birth to a child
放火	set fire	讲话	speaking

翻译练习－ Translation

1. 我有点不舒服，你能替我写个病假条吗？

2. 我们谁也/都没想到他不会说汉语。

3. 我的手机没电了，没想到你的也没电了。我们怎么找人来帮助我们呢？

4. 就人口而言，中国是全球人口最多的国家。

5. ── 小王为什么穿得这么正式？

   ── 谁知道呢！他最近一直很怪。

6. 我夏天去了新疆，那儿的烤羊肉真好吃/香。

Lesson 37

听力练习－ Listening Practice

1.b　2.a　3.a　4.c　5.b　6.a　7.c　8.b

语法练习－ Grammar Practice

单项选择

1.c　2.c　3.b　4.c　5.a　6.c　7.b　8.a

选词填空

时候、到、问、别人、后来、怎么、规定、吹、一点儿、就是

认字识词－ Words with Known Characters

1.	退休	retire	反对	against, oppose
	误会	mistake	反义词	antonym
	错误	error	同义词	synonym
	靠近	come near	同音词	homophone
	到达	arrive	老伴儿	old spouse

2.

干洗	dry cleaning	慢跑	jogging
高考	university entrance exam	大选	gerenal election
巧遇	bump into sb.	冷烫	cold perm (hair)
单打	play singles	双打	double play
早婚	early marriage	晚婚	late marriage
紧靠	close by, next to	白吃	freeload

翻译练习－Translation

1. 昨天我在老王家的时候，看见他爷爷穿袍子留辫子的照片了。

2. 今天早上公路上没有公共汽车，你知道是怎么回事吗？

3. 一开始我不太懂那儿的人（说话）的口音，现在我已经习惯了。

4. 你说什么？难道他今天早上靠左边开车去上班了？

5. 这是一个多元的世界，在有的国家里，一个男人可以有好几个太太。

6. 我在南非居住了五年。在那里，我也交了很多朋友。

Lesson 38

听力练习－Listening Practice

1.a　2.c　3.b　4.c　5.b　6.c　7.c　8.a

语法练习－Grammar Practice

单项选择

1.a　2.a　3.b　4.b　5.b　6.c　7.b　8.c

选词填空

招聘、精通、没想到、居然、广告、马上、使用、熟练、种、看着

认字识词－Words with Known Characters

1.

西瓜	watermelon	建造	build
兰花	orchid	大众	masses, popular
事实	fact	高科技	high tech
传球	pass ball	资本	capital
皇上	emperor	胜利	victory

2.	中国造	made in China	心算	mental calculation
	口吃	stammer	自助	self-service
	自主	independence	师传	passed on by master
	手写	hand written	友爱	affection, (platonic) love
	云游	roam	日出	sunrise
	笔录	notes	鱼死网破	a life-or-death struggle

翻译练习－ Translation

1. 我没想到他这么喜欢吹牛。

2. 我听说你们公司在招聘实习生，我对此/这很感兴趣。

3. 我们老师很有才华，她画儿画得很好。

4. 我去年去/访问了中国很多地方，中国人都非常热情。

5. 你有什么爱好/你的爱好是什么？我喜欢爬山、骑马、跳舞和看书。

6. 我有很多银行工作经验，我相信我能胜任这个工作。

Lesson 39

听力练习－ Listening Practice

1.a   2.c   3.a   4.b   5.c   6.b   7.a   8.b

语法练习 － Grammar Practice

单项选择

1.a   2.c   3.a   4.a   5.b   6.c   7.a   8.b

选词填空

快、也、过、往年、一、没有、来、不必、还是、与其

认字识词－ Words with Known Characters

1.	故事	story	陪同	accompany
	理由	reason	骗子	cheat, con-man
	鞋刷	shoe brush	姑姑	aunt
	随和	easy-going	购买	purchase
	随身听	walkman	药膏	ointment

2.

改变	change	说明	explain
放大	amplify	完成	accomplish
识破	seen through	拉平	flatten out
表明	show	推进	push on
刷新	break record / renovate	说开	speak out
登高	climb	跌倒	fall down

翻译练习－ Translation

1. 被他骗了几次以后，我们再也不（相）信他说的话了/他说什么我们都不信了。

2. 英国许多商店一月份都打折（卖它们的商品）。

3. 我父母/爸爸妈妈喜欢去自由市场买东西，因为那儿的东西物美价廉。

4. 下星期我们一定见（一）面。是我去你那儿还是你来我这儿？

5. 她故意买了这条大连衣裙，因为她听说今年夏天很流行这种款式/因为她听说这是今年夏天流行的款式。

6. 她是我们学校里最漂亮的姑娘，追她的小伙子多得不得了。

Lesson 40

听力练习－ Listening Practice

1.b　2.b　3.a　4.a　5.b　6.a　7.c　8.c

语法练习－ Grammar Practice

单项选择

1.b　2.c　3.a　4.b　5.c　6.a　7.c　8.a

选词填空

住下、因此、离开、仔细地、真的、才、名称、虽然、所在、写着

认字识词－ Words with Known Characters

1.

博士	doctor(PhD)	帝国	empire
教堂	church	模式	mode
米色	cream colour	如何	how

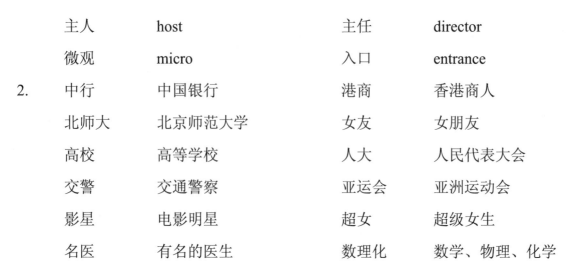

	主人	host		主任	director
	微观	micro		入口	entrance
2.	中行	中国银行		港商	香港商人
	北师大	北京师范大学		女友	女朋友
	高校	高等学校		人大	人民代表大会
	交警	交通警察		亚运会	亚洲运动会
	影星	电影明星		超女	超级女生
	名医	有名的医生		数理化	数学、物理、化学

翻译练习－Translation

1. 检查以前， 医生禁止你吃任何东西。

2. 总理今天要为他在人民大会堂举行一个欢迎宴会。

3. 那个国家的东西很贵，没有几千美元你是不能去那儿度假的。

4. 这个建筑群大约占地5000平方米。

5. 你知道中国末代/最后一个皇帝的名字吗？

6. 虽然他所说的不都是真的，但我想他不是故意骗你的。

附录五 Appendix 5

词汇表 Chinese - English Vocabulary List

阿	ā		noun prefix	37
阿拉伯	Ālābó	专名	Arab, Arabic	37
爱好	àihào	名	hobby	38
安	ān	形/动	peaceful; arrange	40
按	àn	介	by	34
按照	ànzhào	介	according to	34
百货大楼	bǎihuò dàlóu	名	department store	39
般	bān	名	type; like	31
板	bǎn	名	plank	35
板寸	bǎncùn	名	cropped hair	35
办	bàn	动	do, handle	31
办公室	bàngōngshì	名	office	31
办理	bànlǐ	动	deal with, process	31
伴	bàn	名	companion	37
棒	bàng	形/名	very good (colloquial); bat, stick	32
棒球	bàngqiú	名	baseball	32
包裹	bāoguǒ	名	parcel	34
保存	bǎocún	动	preserve	40
保价	bǎojià	名	value insurance	34
报到	bàodào	动	report one's arrival or presence	31
被	bèi	名	quilt	34
被套	bèitào	名	quilt cover	34
笨	bèn	形	stupid, slow	36
比较	bǐjiào	副	relatively	33
比如	bǐrú	动	give an example; for instance	34
毕	bì	动	complete	38
必	bì	情动	have to	34
必要	bìyào	形	necessary	39
必须	bìxū	情动	must	34
毕业	bìyè	动	graduate	38
辫	biàn	名	plaits, pigtail	37
辫子	biànzi	名	plaits, pigtail	37
标	biāo	名/动	mark	33
标记	biāojì	名	mark	33
表达	biǎodá	动/名	express	37

表格	biǎogé	名	forms	31
宾	bīn	名	guest	35
伯	bó	名	uncle	37
博	bó	形	vast, extensive	40
博物馆	bówùguǎn	名	museum	40
部	bù	名	department; part; section	32
不得了	bùdéliǎo	副	(colloquial) very much	39
不管	bùguǎn	连	no matter	33
不好意思	bù hǎo yìsi	形	embarrassed	32
不见得	bújiànde	副	not necessarily	37
不仅	bùjǐn	连	not only	32
不仅…而且	bùjǐn…érqiě		not only…but also…	32
不然	bùrán	连	otherwise, if not	31
不同	bùtóng	名	different	36
才	cái	名	talent	38
才华	cáihuá	名	talent	38
参观	cānguān	动	visit and tour around (a place)	40
册	cè	名	volume, book	31
查询	cháxún	动	ask; seek information	34
偿	cháng	动	return; satisfy	34
长裙	chángqún	名	long skirt	39
抄	chāo	动	copy	36
超短裙	chāoduǎnqún	名	mini skirt	39
超市	chāoshì	名	supermarket	33
称	chēng	动	weigh; be called as; scale	34
称	chēng	动	call; say	40
称为	chēngwéi	动	be called as	40
城楼	chénglóu	名	rostrum	40
成为	chéngwéi	动	become	33
迟	chí	形	late	32
迟到	chídào	动	arrive late	32
吃力	chīlì	形	entail strenuous effort	37
处	chù	名	place; department	33
传	chuán	动	pass on	38
传真	chuánzhēn	名	fax	38
床单	chuángdān	名	bed sheet	34
出入	chūrù	动	in and out; entry and exit	40
出色	chūsè	形	outstanding	35
出众	chūzhòng	形	outstanding	38

吹	chuī	动	blow (style the hair)	35
聪	cōng	形	clever	36
聪明	cōngming	形	intelligent, clever	36
存	cún	动	deposit	33
寸	cùn	名	Chinese inch	35
错误	cuòwù	名	mistake, wrong	37
达	dá	动	reach	37
打听	dǎting	动	make an enquiry	35
打折	dǎ zhé	动	give discount	39
大部分	dàbùfen	名	most of	32
大街	dàjiē	名	broadway; avenue	35
大量	dàliàng	副	a great deal	31
大娘	dàniáng	名	aunty/granny	39
大约	dàyuē	副	approximately	31
单	dān	形/名	single; bill	33
单	dān	名	sheet	34
单裤	dānkù	名	trousers (without padding)	39
单元	dānyuán	名	unit; module	33
当场	dāngchǎng	副	on the spot	39
当年	dāngnián	名	at that time (year)	34
到底	dàodǐ	副	to the end	34
盗	dào	动	steal	33
盗用	dàoyòng	动	embezzle	33
帝	dì	名	emperor, imperial	40
地址	dìzhǐ	名	address	33
调	diào	名	intonation, tone	37
订	dìng	动	book; subscribe	31
定期	dìngqī	名	fixed term	33
丢	diū	动	lose	33
东单	Dōngdān	专名	a shopping street in Beijing	35
洞	dòng	名	hole	39
读	dú	动	read	31
短	duǎn	形	short	35
锻	duàn	动	forge	32
锻炼	duànliàn	动	have physical training	32
队	duì	名	team	32
队员	duìyuán	名	member of a competition team	32
对内	duì nèi	介宾结构	internal	36
对外	duì wài	介宾结构	external	36

多元	duōyuán	形	multiple	37
而	ér	连	and; just	32
而且	érqiě	连	but also	32
反	fǎn	形	opposite; against	37
发	fà	名	hair	35
发廊	fàláng	名	hair salon	35
发型	fàxíng	名	hair style	35
范	fàn	名	limits	36
范围	fànwéi	名	scope, range	36
方便	fāngbiàn	形	convenient	32
方法	fāngfǎ	名	method	36
方式	fāngshì	名	manner; approach	32
访	fǎng	动	visit	40
放心	fàngxīn	形	rest assure of	33
肥	féi	名/形	fat	39
肥皂	féizào	名	soap	39
分行	fēnháng	名	branch	38
份	fèn	名	share	33
份	fèn	量	for a job or newspapers or magazine	38
封	fēng	动/量	seal; M.W for letter	37
风险	fēngxiǎn	名	risk	38
府	fǔ	名	mansion	35
附	fù	动	attach	37
附上	fùshàng	动	add, attach	37
该	gāi	代	this, that	35
改	gǎi	动	change ,correct	32
改变	gǎibiàn	动	change	32
港	gǎng	名	harbour	33
港币	Gǎngbì	专名	Hong Kong dollar	33
膏	gāo	名	paste	39
告	gào	动	tell	36
告诉	gàosu	动	tell	36
格	gé	名	square formed by cross lines; check	31
格式	géshì	名	format	37
格外	géwài	副	especially	40
更加	gèngjiā	副	even more	36
宫	gōng	名	palace	40
公开	gōngkāi	动	make public	36
工资	gōngzī	名	salary	38

狗熊	gǒuxióng	名	black bear; a coward	39
狗不理包子	Gǒubùlǐ bāozi	专名	a well known brand of steamed dumpling in Tianjin	37
购	gòu	动	purchase	39
购物	gòuwù	动/名	(go) shopping	39
姑	gū	名	auntie (paternal side)	39
姑娘	gūniang	名	girl	39
古	gǔ	形	ancient	40
古代	gǔdài	名	ancient times	40
古建筑群	gǔjiànzhùqún	名	a cluster of ancient architecture	40
故	gù	副	on purpose; old	39
故宫	gùgōng	名	Imperial Palace	40
故意	gùyì	副	intentionally	39
顾	gù	动	visit; see	35
顾客	gùkè	名	customer	35
挂号	guàhào	名/动	register	34
挂念	guàniàn	动	worry about; concern	37
关于	guānyú	介	about	36
观	guān	动	look, observe	40
管	guǎn	动	mind; manage	33
管理	guǎnlǐ	名/动	management	38
惯	guàn	动	spoil; be used to	37
广场	guǎngchǎng	名	a square	32
广告	guǎnggào	名	advertisement	36
逛	guàng	动	walk about	39
规	guī	名/动	rule	34
规定	guīdìng	名/动	stipulation	34
规模	guīmó	名	scale	40
国籍	guójí	名	nationality	38
国际	guójì	名	international	33
裹	guǒ	名/动	parcel; wrap	34
过冬	guò dōng	动	go through winter	39
海德	Hǎidé	专名	Hyde (transliteration)	38
海运	hǎiyùn	名	transport by sea	34
航天	hángtiān	名	aerospace	35
航天员	hángtiānyuán	名	astronaut	35
好	hào	动	like, love	37
好客	hàokè	形	be hospitable	37
何	hé	名	which	40
华	huá	名	glamour	38

皇	huáng	名/形	emperor; royal	38
皇帝	huángdì	名	emperor	40
皇宫	huánggōng	名	royal palace	40
皇家	huángjiā	名	royal family	38
惠	huì	动	benefit	39
活	huó	动/形	live; alive	32
活动	huódòng	动/名	exercise; activity	32
活期	huóqī	名	current (account)	33
伙	huǒ	名	mate	37
伙伴	huǒbàn	名	partner	37
货	huò	名	commodity; goods	33
货币	huòbì	名	currency	33
获	huò	动	capture, reap	37
或	huò	连	or	34
或者	huòzhě	连	or	39
籍	jí	名	native town; record	38
急	jí	形	pressing	36
己	jǐ	代.	oneself	36
纪	jì	动	record	34
纪念	jìniàn	名/动	commemorate	34
纪念堂	jìniàntáng	名	memorial hall	40
技	jì	名	skill; technology	38
技能	jìnéng	名	skill	38
际	jì	名	border, boundary	33
价	jià	名	value; price	34
检	jiǎn	动	inspect	34
检查	jiǎnchá	动	inspect; check	34
剪	jiǎn	动	cut	35
建	jiàn	动	build	38
建筑	jiànzhù	名	architecture	38
健	jiàn	形	healthy	31
健康	jiànkāng	形	healthy	37
健身	jiànshēng	名/动	keep healthy	32
健身房	jiànshēnfáng	名	gym	32
将	jiāng	副	be going to	36
讲	jiǎng	动	talk	36
讲课	jiǎng kè	动	give lecture	37
讲座	jiǎngzuò	名	open lecture	36
奖	jiǎng	名/动	award; reward	33

奖学金	jiǎngxuéjīn	名	scholarship	33
交费	jiāofèi	动	pay fees	31
较	jiào	副	compared with; comparably	33
教练	jiàoliàn	名	coach, trainer	32
街	jiē	名	street	35
节	jié	量	period; session	32
结束	jiéshù	动	finish, end	40
结算	jiésuàn	名/动	settle (a transaction) by (a currency)	33
借记卡	jièjìkǎ	名	debit card	33
界	jiè	名	boundary	37
紧	jǐn	形	tight	36
紧急	jǐnjí	形	urgent	36
仅	jǐn	副	only	32
进修	jìnxiū	动/名	engage in advanced studies	31
禁	jìn	动	forbid	40
禁地	jìndì	名	forbidden place	40
禁止	jìnzhǐ	动	forbid	40
精	jīng	形	smart	35
精神	jīngshen	形/名	smart looking, spirit	35
精	jīng	形/名	perfect; essence	38
精通	jīngtōng	动/形	be proficient in	38
经历	jīnglì	名/动	experience	38
景	jǐng	名	scene	40
景点	jǐngdiǎn	名	places of interest	40
井	jǐng	名	well	35
敬	jìng	动	honour	36
敬礼	jìnglǐ	名/动	salute	36
旧	jiù	形	old (not for age)	33
就业	jiùyè	名/动	to get a job; obtain employment	36
就座	jiùzuò	动	be seated	36
居	jū	动	live	37
居然	jūrán	副	unexpectedly	38
居住	jūzhù	名/动	habitation; live	37
局	jú	名	bureau	34
举	jǔ	动	hold up	40
举行	jǔxíng	动	hold; take place	40
俱	jù	形	all, complete	32
俱乐部	jùlèbù	名	club	32
卡拉OK	kālā-OK	名	karioke	38

开业	kāiyè	动/名	(business) start	35
康	kāng	形	healthy; rich	37
靠	kào	介/动	keep to; rely on	37
科	kē	名	branch; subject	31
空调	kōngtiáo	名	air conditioning	31
空运	kōngyùn	名	transport by air	34
口头	kǒutóu	形	oral	36
夸	kuā	动	exaggerate; praise	38
夸张	kuāzhāng	动	exaggerate	38
啦	la	助	a phrase-final particle（fusion of le +a）	37
拉	lā	动	pull	36
拉肚子	lādùzi	动/名	have diarrhoea	36
来访	láifǎng	动	come and visit	40
来自	láizì	动+介	come from	31
兰	lán	名	orchid	38
览	lǎn	动	browse	31
廊	láng	名	corridor, veranda	35
老王卖瓜，自卖自夸			boat of one's own products	38
老字号	lǎozìhào	名	long established brand (shop)	35
李健	Lǐ Jiàn	专名	a Chinese name	31
理发	lǐfà	动	hair cut	35
理发店	lǐfàdiàn	名	barber's shop/hair dresser's	35
理科	lǐkē	名	science (subjects of study)	31
历法	lìfǎ	名	time calculation method	34
利息	lìxī	名	interest	33
例	lì	名	instance	36
例外	lìwài	名	exception	37
例子	lìzi	名	example	36
力量	lìliàng	名	strength	31
联	lián	动	connect	33
联系	liánxì	动	contact	33
连剪带吹	liánjiǎn dàichuī		cut and blow (hair)	35
连忙	liánmáng	副	hurriedly	39
连衣裙	liányīqún	名	long dress	39
廉	lián	形	cheap	39
炼	liàn	动	refine	32
量	liàng	名	capacity; quantity	31
列	liè	名	rank	33
零起点	língqǐdiǎn	名	zero start	31

另	lìng	副/代	other, another	33
另外	lìngwài	副	besides	33
轮	lún	动	take turns	35
轮	lún	名	wheel	34
轮船	lúnchuán	名	ship steamer	34
录取	lùqǔ	动/名	admission; admit (on a programme)	31
马来西亚	Mǎláixīyà	专名	Malaysia	31
骂	mà	动	curse, scold	39
毛主席	Máo Zhǔxí	专名	Chairman Mao	40
每	měi	代	every, each	32
美白	Měibái	专名	Meibai（a name）	35
美发	měifà	动/名	do one's hair	35
美观大方	měiguān-dàfāng		with nice and elegant appearance	39
美容	měiróng	名/动	art of make-up	35
门	mén	量	for a subject of study	32
米	mǐ	量/名	meter, rice	40
密	mì	名/形	secrecy, secret	33
密码	mìmǎ	名	pin number	33
名列	míngliè	动	list as	33
模	mó	名	mode	40
目	mù	名	list; eye	32
目录	mùlù	名	table of contents, catalogue	32
目前	mùqián	副	now	38
奶奶	nǎinai	名	grandma	34
难道	nándào	副	emphatic word in a question	37
内	nèi	名	inner part	36
内部	nèibù	名	internal; interior	36
能力	nénglì	名	capability	38
念	niàn	动	miss; study; read	34
娘	niáng	名	mother	39
牛皮大王	niúpí dàwáng	名	(colloquial) braggart	38
牛仔裤	niúzǎikù	名	jeans	39
暖气	nuǎnqì	名	central heating	39
女士	nǚshì	名	lady	35
爬山	pá shān	名/动	mountain climb	38
排	pái	动/名	queue; row	35
排队	pái duì	动	queue	35
乒	pāng	名	onomatopoeic character	32
袍子	páozi	名	robe	37

CHINESE IN STEPS
Appendices

赔	péi	动	compensate	34
赔偿	péicháng	动	compensate	34
陪	péi	动	accompany	39
骗	piàn	动	cheat, deceive	39
品种	pǐnzhǒng	名	kinds, types	33
聘	pìn	动	invite to engage	38
乓	pīng	名	onomatopoeic character	32
乒乓球	pīngpāngqiú	名	table tennis	32
平	píng	形	even, level	34
平常	píngcháng	形	common; ordinary	34
平方米	píngfāngmǐ	名	square metre	40
平头	píngtóu	名	cropped hair	35
其	qí	代	that; particle	39
齐	qí	动	full, complete	39
齐全	qíquán	形	complete	39
骑马	qí mǎ	名/动	horse riding	38
起点	qǐdiǎn	名	starting point	31
起名	qǐmíng	动/名	name	31
签	qiān	动	sign	36
千万	qiānwàn	副		39
且	qiě	连	and; but also	32
切	qiè	动	be suitable; be close to	37
亲	qīn	形	next of kin; kiss	37
亲爱的	qīn'ài de		dear; my dear	37
青年人	qīngniánrén	名	the youth	32
请假	qǐngjià	动/名	ask for leave	36
请假条	qǐngjià tiáo	名	written request for leave/absence	36
求职信	qiúzhí xìn	名	application letter	38
区	qū	名	area	36
区别	qūbié	名	difference	36
取	qú	动	get, take	31
全	quán	形	whole; complete	37
全部	quánbù	副	completely	37
群	qún	名/量	cluster, group	40
染	rǎn	动	(to) colour	35
染发	rǎnfà	动/名	colour hair	35
热情	rèqíng	形	warm; welcome	38
任	rèn	动	act as	38
任何	rènhé	名	any	40

人民大会堂	Rénmín Dàhuìtáng	专名	The Great Hall of the People	40
日期	rìqī	名	date	37
如	rú	连	if; like	31
如此	rúcǐ	副	just like this; so, such	37
如果	rúguǒ	连	if	31
商量	shāngliang	动/名	consult, discuss	32
商业	shāngyè	名	commercial; business	36
设	shè	动	set up	31
设施	shèshī	名	facilities	31
神	shén	名	spirit; god	35
身	shēn	名	body	32
身份	shénfen	名	identity, postition	33
身份证	shēnfènzhèng	名	ID card	33
身体	shēntǐ	名	body	32
胜	shèng	名/动	win	38
胜任	shèngrèn	动	capable of the job	38
匙	shi/chí	名	key; spoon	31
施	shī	名/动	carry out; exert	31
食	shí	名	food; eat	37
食物	shíwù	名	food	37
实	shí	形	actual, real	38
实习	shíxí	动	do intern work	38
实习生	shíxíshēng	名	intern	38
使用	shǐyòng	动	utilise; use	33
世	shì	名	world	37
世界	shìjiè	名	world	37
士	shì	名	person	35
事先	shìxiān	副	beforehand; in advance	36
市中心	shìzhōngxīn	名	city centre	35
收获	shōuhuò	名	gains, harvest	37
手工	shǒugōng	名	handwork, handmade	34
手续	shǒuxù	名	procedure	31
输	shū	名/动	transport	34
书法	shūfǎ	名	calligraphy	32
书面	shūmiàn	形	written	36
熟	shú/shóu	形	cooked; familiar	36
熟悉	shúxi	动/形	be familiar with	38
属	shǔ	动	be born in the year of; belong to	34
属相	shǔxiàng	名	zodiac animal	34

数	shù	名	number	31
数学	shùxué	名	maths	31
束	shù	动	tie; control	40
术	shù	名	art; skill	32
刷	shuā	名/动	brush	39
帅	shuài	形	smart; handsome	35
睡衣	shuìyī	名	pyjama	34
思	sī	动	think; miss	31
私	sī	形	private, personal	32
私人	sīrén	形	private, personal	32
死	sǐ	形/动	dead, die, death	32
死期	sǐqī	名	fixed term (deposit account)	33
死去活来	sǐqù-huólái		very much; a great deal	39
四联	Sìlián	专名	a name of a barber's shop	35
苏	Sū	名	a surname	38
苏格兰	Sūgélán	专名	Scotland	38
诉	sù	动	tell	36
随	suí	动	follow	39
随便	suíbiàn	副	casually; as you like	39
所	suǒ	助	which, that	40
所在	suǒzài	名	place; place where something exists	40
堂	táng	名	hall	40
烫	tàng	动	scald, burn	35
烫发	tàngfà	动/名	perm one's hair	35
套	tào	名	cover;（量）a set of	34
特级	tèjí	形	special grade/class; superfine	35
体	tǐ	名	body	32
替	tì	动/介	substitute; on behalf of	36
天安门	Tiān'ānmén	专名	Tian'anmen	40
天帝	tiāndì	名	celestial emperor (Emperor of the Heaven)	40
天文学	tiānwénxué	名	astronomy	40
调	tiáo	动	adjust	31
条	tiáo	名	note	36
条件	tiáojiàn	名	condition	37
停止	tíngzhǐ	动	stop	40
同	tóng	形	identical	36
同学	tóngxué	名	classmate, schoolmate	37
同志	tóngzhì	名	comrade	40
通告	tōnggào	名	public notice, announcement	36

通票	tōngpiào	名	a ticket for all entries	40
通知	tōngzhī	名	notice	36
通知书	tōngzhīshū	名	admission letter	31
透	tòu	动/形	permeate; transparent	33
透支	tòuzhī	动/名	overdraft	33
推	tuī	动	push	38
推销	tuīxiāo	动	promote; market	38
退	tuì	动	send back, return, retreat	37
外宾	wàibīn	名	foreign guest	40
万	wàn	数	ten thousand	39
王小明	Wáng Xiǎomíng	专名	a Chinese name	31
王府井	Wángfǔjǐng	专名	a shopping street in Beijing	35
往	wǎng	介	toward	33
往来账户	wǎnglái zhànghù	名	current account	33
为	wéi	动	be; become	31
围	wéi	名/动	all round; surround	36
微	wéi	形	small, tiny	40
位于	wèi yú	动	situated at/in	35
文科	wénkē	名	liberal arts	31
武	wǔ	名/形	military	32
武术	wǔshù	名	martial art	32
误	wù	名	error	37
误以为	wù yǐwéi		mistake for	37
物美价廉	wùměi-jiàlián		(product) cheap but good	39
西单	Xīdān	专名	a shopping street in Beijing	35
习惯	xíguàn	动/名	be used to, habit	37
席	xí	名	seat	40
悉	xī	动	know	38
系列	xìliè	名	series; serial	33
先进	xiānjìn	形	advanced	31
显	xiǎn	动	reveal, show	35
显眼	xiǎnyǎn	形	conspicuous	35
现成	xiànchéng	形	ready-made	36
现存	xiàncún	形	currently existing, surviving	40
香	xiāng	形	fragrant	33
香港	Xiānggǎng	专名	Hong Kong	33
香皂	xiāngzào	名	soap with fragrance	39
相	xiāng		each other	34
相差	xiāngchà	动	differ from each other	34

CHINESE IN STEPS

Appendices

相反	xiāngfǎn	形	opposite, contrary;	37
相同	xiāngtóng	名	identical, same	36
销	xiāo	动	sell	38
小伙子	xiǎohuǒzi	名	young lad	39
校队	xiàoduì	名	school/college team	32
新鲜	xīnxiān	形	fresh	36
信封	xìnfēng	名	envelope	37
信箱	xìnxiāng	名	letter box	38
信用	xìnyòng	名	credit	33
信用卡	xìnyòngkǎ	名	credit card	33
型	xíng	名	style; shape; model	35
修	xiū	动	repair; study	31
绣	xiù	动	embroider	34
绣花	xiùhuā	名/动	embroidery	34
须	xū	情动	must	34
续	xù	动	continue	31
选	xuǎn	动	select	32
选修	xuǎnxiū	动/名	select an optional course	32
学历	xuélì	名	education qualification	38
学名	xuémíng	名	scientific name, formal name	32
学生会	xuéshēnghuì	名	student union	36
学生证	xuéshēngzhèng	名	student card	32
学位	xuéwèi	名	(academic) degree	31
询	xún	动	ask	34
牙膏	yágāo	名	toothpaste	39
宴	yàn	名	formal meal, banquet	40
阳	yáng	名	Sun; masculine	34
羊	yáng	名	goat, sheep	36
羊肉	yángròu	名	roast lamb	36
阳历	yánglì	名	solar calendar; Gregory calendar	34
宴会	yànhuì	名	banquet	40
钥	yào	名	keys	31
钥匙	yàoshi	名	keys	31
牙刷	yáshuā	名	tooth brush	39
业务	yèwù	名	business	35
仪	yí	名	ceremony; appearance	40
仪式	yíshì	名	rite, ceremony	40
以…（能力）	yǐ…nénglì		by the capability of	38
一切	yíqiè	代	every, all	37

一般	yìbān	形	ordinary; common	31
一开始	yìkāishǐ		at the beginning	37
意	yì	名	desire	38
意思	yìsi	名	meaning	31
因而	yīn'ér	连	thus, therefore	40
阴历	yīnlì	名	Chinese lunar calendar	34
引	yīn	动	guide	35
引起	yǐnqǐ	动	cause, give rise to	35
用户	yònghù	名	users; client	34
优	yōu	形	excellent	39
优惠价	yōuhuìjià	名	preferential price	39
由	yóu	动/介	let; by	39
邮	yóu	名	post	34
邮票	yóupiào	名	stamp	34
邮局	yóujú	名	post office	34
有意者	yǒuyìzhě		person who is interested	38
于	yú	介	at, in; a surname	35
于爱华	Yú Àihuá	专名	a Chinese name	37
与	yǔ	连	with	39
与其…不如	yǔqí...bùrú	连	rather…than…	39
语调	yǔdiào	名	intonation	37
语音	yǔyīn	名	pronunciation	37
预订	yùdìng	动	book (a place, ticket etc) in advance	31
元	yuán	名	unit	33
元	yuán	名	element, component	37
原	yuán	副	original	34
原来	yuánlái	副	originally	34
原因	yuányīn	名	cause, reason	36
约	yuē	副/动	about; make an appointment	31
阅	yuè	动	read	31
阅览室	yuèlǎnshì	名	reading room	31
月份	yuèfen	名	month	34
运	yùn	动	transport	34
运输	yùnshū	动	transport; lose	34
杂	zá	形	mixed	31
杂志	zázhì	名	magazine	31
仔	zǎi	名	cub; child	39
皂	zào	名	soap	39
占	zhàn	动	occupy	40

占地	zhàndì	动	occupy an area of	40
账	zhàng	名	account	33
账户	zhànghù	名	account	33
招	zhāo	动	attract	38
招聘	zhāopìn	动	recruit	38
折	zhé	名/动	discount; fold; break	39
者	zhě	名	suffix for person	38
真龙天子	zhēnlóng tiānzǐ	名	real son of the dragon (emperor)	40
证	zhèng	名	certificate, card; proof	32
正式	zhèngshì	形	formal	36
支	zhī	动	pay	33
之	zhī		of; object substitute	35
之一	zhī yī		one of	35
职	zhí	名	profession	33
职员	zhíyuán	名	clerk	33
止	zhǐ	动	stop	40
址	zhǐ	名	site	33
至	zhì	介	to	38
至今	zhìjīn	副	up to now	38
志	zhì	名	records	31
制品	zhìpǐn	名	products	34
中天	zhōngyiān	名	centre of cosmos	40
中文系	Zhōngwénxì	名	department of Chinese language and literature	31
重要	zhòngyòo	形	important	32
众	zhòng	名	mass	38
主	zhǔ	形	main	40
祝	zhù	动	wish	37
筑	zhù	动	construct	38
住处	zhùchù	名	dwelling	33
注	zhù	动	record, register	31
注册	zhùcè	动/名	register	31
注意	zhùyì	动/名	notice; attention	35
装	zhuāng	动	put; hold	39
追	zhuī	动	court; go after	39
准	zhǔn	动/形	allow; accurate; punctual	36
准假	zhǔn jià	动	authorize the leave	36
资	zī	名	capital	38
紫禁城	Zǐjìnchéng	专名	Forbidden City	40
紫微星	Zǐwēixīng	专名	North Star	40

自己	zìjǐ	代	oneself	36
自动	zìdòng	形/副	automatic	32
自觉	zìjué	形	self-conscious	32
自由市场	zìyóu shìchǎng	名	free market	39
字样	zìyàng	名	written expressions	36
总理	zǒnglǐ	名	premier, prime minister	40
走神	zǒushén	动	become distracted or absent minded	39
尊	zūn	动	respect	36
尊敬	zūnjìng	名/动	respect	36

附录六　Appendix 6

词汇表　English - Chinese Vocabulary List

a cluster of ancient architecture	古建筑群	gǔ jiànzhùqún	名	40
a great deal	大量	dàliàng	副	31
a Chinese name	李健	Lǐ Jiàn	专名	31
a Chinese name	王小明	Wáng Xiǎomíng	专名	31
a Chinese name	于爱华	Yú Àihuá	专名	37
a Chinese surname	苏	Sū	名	38
a name of a barber's shop	美白	Měibái	专名	35
a name of a barber's shop	四联	Sìlián	专名	35
a shopping street in Beijing	东单	Dōngdān	专名	35
a shopping street in Beijing	西单	Xīdān	专名	35
a shopping street in Beijing	王府井	Wángfǔjǐng	专名	35
application letter	求职信	qiúzhíxìn	名	38
a phrase-final particle（fusion of le + a）	啦	la	助	37
a ticket for all entries	通票	tōngpiào	名	40
a well known brand of steamed dumpling in Tianjin	狗不理包子	Gǒubùlǐ bāozi	专名	37
a square	广场	guǎngchǎng	名	32
about	关于	guānyú	介	36
about; make an appointment	约	yuē	副/动	31
accompany	陪	péi	动	39
according to	按照	ànzhào	介	34
account	账	zhàng	名	33
account	账户	zhànghù	名	33
act as	任	rèn	动	38
actual, real	实	shí	形	38
add, attach	附上	fùshàng	动	37
address	地址	dìzhǐ	名	33
adjust	调	tiáo	动	31
admission letter	通知书	tōngzhīshū	名	31
admission; admit (on a programme)	录取	lùqǔ	动/名	31
advanced	先进	xiānjìn	形	31
advertisement	广告	guǎnggào	名	36
aerospace	航天	hángtiān	名	35
air conditioning	空调	kōngtiáo	名	31
all round; surround	围	wéi	名/动	36
all, complete	俱	jù	形	32

allow; accurate; punctual	准	zhǔn	动/形	36
ancient	古	gǔ	形	40
ancient times	古代	gǔdài	名	40
and; but also	且	qiě	连	32
and; just	而	ér	连	32
any	任何	rènhé	名	40
approximately	大约	dàyuē	副	31
Arab, Arabic	阿拉伯	Ālābó	专名	37
architecture	建筑	jiànzhù	名	38
area	区	qū	名	36
arrive late	迟到	chídào	动	32
art of make-up	美容	měiróng	名/动	35
art; skill	术	shù	名	32
ask	询	xún	动	34
ask for leave	请假	qǐngjià	动/名	36
ask; seek information	查询	cháxún	动	34
astronaut	航天员	hángtiānyuán	名	35
astronomy	天文学	tiānwénxué	名	40
at that time (year)	当年	dāngnián	名	34
at the beginning	一开始	yìkāishǐ		37
at, in; a surname	于	yú	介	35
attach	附	fù	动	37
attract	招	zhāo	动	38
auntie (paternal side)	姑	gū	名	39
aunty/granny	大娘	dàniáng	名	39
authorize the leave	准假	zhǔnjià	动	36
automatic	自动	zìdòng	形/副	32
award; reward	奖	jiǎng	名/动	33
banquet	宴会	yànhuì	名	40
barber's shop/hair dresser's	理发店	lǐfàdiàn	名	35
baseball	棒球	bàngqiú	名	32
be born in the year of ; belong to	属	shǔ	动	34
be called as	称为	chēngwéi	动	40
be familiar with	熟悉	shúxi	动/形	38
be going to	将	jiāng	副	36
be hospitable	好客	hàokè	形	37
be proficient in	精通	jīngtōng	动/形	38
be seated	就座	jiùzuò	动	36
be suitable; be close to	切	qiè	动	37

be used to, habit	习惯	xíguàn	动/名	37
be; become	为	wéi	动	31
become	成为	chéngwéi	动	33
become distracted or absent minded	走神	zǒushén	动	39
bed sheet	床单	chuángdān	名	34
beforehand; in advance	事先	shìxiān	副	36
benefit	惠	huì	动	39
besides	另外	lìngwài	副	33
black bear; a coward	狗熊	gǒuxióng	名	39
blow (style the hair)	吹	chuī	动	35
boat of one's own products	老王卖瓜，自卖自夸			38
body	身	shēn	名	32
body	体	tǐ	名	32
body	身体	shēntǐ	名	32
book; subscribe	订	dìng	动	31
book (a place, ticket etc) in advance	预订	yùdìng	动	31
border, boundary	际	jì	名	33
boundary	界	jiè	名	37
braggart (colloquial)	牛皮大王	niúpí dàwáng	名	38
branch; subject	科	kē	名	31
branch	分行	fēnháng	名	38
broadway; avenue	大街	dàjiē	名	35
browse	览	lǎn	动	31
brush	刷	shuā	名/动	39
build	建	jiàn	动	38
bureau	局	jú	名	34
business	业务	yèwù	名	35
but also	而且	érqiě	连介	32
by	按	àn	介	34
by the capability of	以…（能力）	yǐ…nénglì		38
call; say	称	chēng	动	40
calligraphy	书法	shūfǎ	名	32
capability	能力	nénglì	名	38
capable of the job	胜任	shèngrèn	动	38
capacity; quantity	量	liàng	名	31
capital	资	zī	名	38
capture, reap	获	huò	动	37
carry out; exert	施	shī	名/动	31
casually; as you like	随便	suíbiàn	副	39

cause, give rise to	引起	yǐnqǐ	动	35
cause, reason	原因	yuányīn	名	36
celestial emperor (Emperor of the Heaven)	天帝	tiāndì	名	40
central heating	暖气	nuǎnqì	名	39
centre of cosmos	中天	zhōngtiān	名	40
ceremony; appearance	仪	yí	名	40
certificate, card; proof	证	zhèng	名	32
Chairman Mao	毛主席	Máo Zhǔxí	专名	40
change, correct	改	gǎi	动	32
change	改变	gǎibiàn	动	32
cheap	廉	lián	形	39
cheap but good (product)	物美价廉	wùměi-jiàlián		39
cheat, deceive	骗	piàn	动	39
Chinese inch	寸	cùn	名	35
Chinese lunar calendar	阴历	yīnlì	名	34
city centre	市中心	shìzhōngxīn	名	35
classmate, schoolmate	同学	tóngxué	名	37
clerk	职员	zhíyuán	名	33
clever	聪	cōng	形	36
club	俱乐部	jùlèbù	名	32
cluster, group	群	qún	名/量	40
coach, trainer	教练	jiàoliàn	名	32
colour hair	染发	rǎnfà	动/名	35
come and visit	来访	láifǎng	动	40
come from	来自	láizì	动+介	31
commercial; business	商业	shāngyè	名	36
commemorate	纪念	jìniàn	名/动	34
commodity; goods	货	huò	名	33
common; ordinary	平常	píngcháng	形	34
companion	伴	bàn	名	37
compared with; comparably	较	jiào	副	33
compensate	赔	péi	动	34
compensate	赔偿	péicháng	动	34
complete	毕	bì	动	38
complete	齐全	qíquán	形	39
completely	全部	quánbù	副	37
comrade	同志	tóngzhì	名	40
condition	条件	tiáojiàn	名	37
connect	联	lián	动	33

conspicuous	显眼	xiǎnyǎn	形	35
construct	筑	zhù	动	38
consult, discuss	商量	shāngliang	动/名	32
contact	联系	liánxì	动	33
continue	续	xù	动	31
convenient	方便	fāngbiàn	形	32
cooked; familiar	熟	shóu/shú	形	36
copy	抄	chāo	动	36
corridor, veranda	廊	láng	名	35
court; go after	追	zhuī	动	39
cover; a set of	套	tào	名	34
credit	信用	xìnyòng	名	33
credit card	信用卡	xìnyòngkǎ	名	33
cropped hair	板寸	bǎncùn	名	35
cropped hair	平头	píngtóu	名	35
cub; child	仔	zǎi	名	39
current (account)	活期	huóqī	名	33
current account	往来账户	wǎnglái zhànghù	名	33
currently existing, surviving	现存	xiàncún	形	40
currency	货币	huòbì	名	33
curse, scold	骂	mà	动	39
customer	顾客	gùkè	名	35
cut	剪	jiǎn	动	35
cut and blow (hair)	连剪带吹	liánjiǎn dàichuī		35
date	日期	rìqī	名	37
dead, die	死	sǐ	形/动	32
deal with, process	办理	bànlǐ	动	31
dear; my dear	亲爱的	qīn'ài de		37
debit card	借记卡	jièjìkǎ	名	33
degree (academic)	学位	xuéwèi	名	31
department store	百货大楼	bǎihuò dàlóu	名	39
department of Chinese language and literature	中文系	Zhōngwénxì	名	31
department; part; section	部	bù	名	32
desire	意	yì	名	38
deposit	存	cún	动	33
difference	区别	qūbié	名	36
different	不同	bùtóng	名	36
differ from each other	相差	xiāngchà	动	34
discount; fold; break	折	zhé	名/动	39

do intern work	实习	shíxí	动	38
do one's hair	美发	měifà	动/名	35
do, handle	办	bàn	动	31
dwelling	住处	zhùchù	名	33
each other	相	xiāng		34
education qualification	学历	xuélì	名	38
element, component	元	yuán	名	37
embarrassed	不好意思	bù hǎo yìsi	形	32
embezzle	盗用	dàoyòng	动	33
embroider	绣	xiù	动	34
embroidery	绣花	xiùhuā	名/动	34
emperor	皇帝	huángdì	名	40
emperor, imperial	帝	dì	名	40
emperor; royal	皇	huáng	名/形	38
emphatic expression for "make sure" or "must"	千万	qiānwàn	副	39
emphatic word in a question	难道	nándào	副	37
to get a job; obtain employment	就业	jiùyè	名/动	36
engage in advanced studies	进修	jìnxiū	动/名	31
entail strenuous effort	吃力	chīlì	形	37
envelope	信封	xìnfēng	名	37
error	误	wù	名	37
especially	格外	géwài	副	40
even, level	平	píng	形	34
even more	更加	gèngjiā	副	36
every, all	一切	yíqiè	代	37
every, each	每	měi	代	32
exaggerate	夸张	kuāzhāng	动	38
exaggerate; praise	夸	kuā	动	38
example	例子	lìzi	名	36
exception	例外	lìwài	名	37
excellent	优	yōu	形	39
exercise; activity	活动	huódòng	动/名	32
experience	经历	jīnglì	名/动	38
express	表达	biǎodá	动/名	37
external	对外	duìwài	介宾结构	36
facilities	设施	shèshī	名	31
fat	肥	féi	名/形	39
fax	传真	chuánzhēn	名	38
finish, end	结束	jiéshù	动	40

fixed term	定期	dìngqā	名	33
fixed term (deposit account)	死期	sǐqī	名	33
follow	随	suí	动	39
food	食物	shíwù	名	37
food; eat	食	shí	名	37
for a job or newspapers or magazine	份	fèn	量	38
for a subject of study	门	mén	量	32
forbid	禁	jìn	动	40
forbid	禁止	jìnzhǐ	动	40
Forbidden City	紫禁城	Zǐjìnchéng	专名	40
forbidden place	禁地	jìndì	名	40
foreign guest	外宾	wàibīn	名	40
forge	锻	duàn	动	32
formal	正式	zhèngshì	形	36
formal meal, banquet	宴	yàn	名	40
format	格式	géshì	名	37
forms	表格	biǎogé	名	31
fragrant	香	xiāng	形	33
free market	自由市场	zìyóu shìchǎng	名	39
fresh	新鲜	xīnxiān	形	36
full, complete	齐	qí	动	39
gains, harvest	收获	shōuhuò	名	37
get, take	取	qǔ	动	31
girl	姑娘	gūniang	名	39
give an example; for instance	比如	bǐrú	动	34
give discount	打折	dǎ zhé	动	39
give lecture	讲课	jiǎng kè	动	37
glamour	华	huá	名	38
go shopping	购物	gòuwù	动/名	39
go through winter	过冬	guò dōng	动	39
goat, sheep	羊	yáng	名	36
graduate	毕业	bìyè	动	38
grandma	奶奶	nǎinai	名	34
guest	宾	bīn	名	35
guide	引	yǐn	动	35
gym	健身房	jiànshēnfáng	名	32
habitation; live	居住	jūzhù	名/动	37
hair	发	fà	名	35
hair cut	理发	lǐfà	动	35

hair salon	发廊	fàláng	名	35
hair style	发型	fàxíng	名	35
hall	堂	táng	名	40
handwork, handmade	手工	shǒugōng	名	34
harbour	港	gǎng	名	33
have diarrhoea	拉肚子	lādùzi	动/名	36
have physical training	锻炼	duànliàn	动	32
have to	必	bì	情动	34
healthy	健	jiàn	形	31
healthy	健康	jiànkāng	形	37
healthy; rich	康	kāng	形	37
hobby	爱好	àihào	名	38
hold up	举	jǔ	动	40
hold; take place	举行	jǔxíng	动	40
hole	洞	dòng	名	39
Hong Kong	香港	Xiānggǎng	专名	33
Hong Kong dollar	港币	Gǎngbì	专名	33
honour	敬	jìng	动	36
horse riding	骑马	qí mǎ	名/动	38
hurriedly	连忙	liánmáng	副	39
Hyde (transliteration)	海德	Hǎidé	专名	38
ID card	身份证	shénfènzhèng	名	33
identical	同	tóng	形	36
identical, same	相同	xiāngtóng	名	36
identity, position	身份	shénfèn	名	33
if	如果	rúguǒ	连	31
if; like	如	rú	连	31
Imperial Palace	故宫	gùgōng	专名	40
important	重要	zhòngyào	形	32
in and out; entry and exit	出入	chūrù	动	40
inner part	内	nèi	名	36
inspect	检	jiǎn	动	34
inspect; check	检查	jiǎnchá	动	34
instance	例	lì	名	36
intelligent, clever	聪明	cōngming	形	36
intentionally	故意	gùyì	副	39
interest	利息	lìxī	名	33
intern	实习生	shíxíshēng	名	38
internal	对内	duì nèi	介宾结构	36

internal; interior	内部	nèibù	名	36
international	国际	guójì	名	33
intonation, tone	调	diào	名	37
intonation	语调	yǔdiào	名	37
invite to engage	聘	pìn	动	38
jeans	牛仔裤	niúzǎikù	名	39
just like this; so, such	如此	rúcǐ	副	37
karioke	卡拉OK	kālā-OK	名	38
keep healthy	健身	jiàn shēn	名/动	32
keep to; rely on	靠	kào	介/动	37
key; spoon	匙	shi /chí	名	31
keys	钥	yào	名	31
keys	钥匙	yàoshi	名	31
kinds, types	品种	pǐnzhǒng	名	33
know	悉	xī	动	38
lady	女士	nǚshì	名	35
late	迟	chí	形	32
let; by	由	yóu	动/介	39
letter box	信箱	xìnxiāng	名	38
liberal arts	文科	wénkē	名	31
like, love	好	hào	动	37
limits	范	fàn	名	36
list; eye	目	mù	名	32
list as	名列	míngliè	动	33
live	居	jū	动	37
live; alive	活	huó	动/形	32
long dress	连衣裙	liányīqún	名	39
long established brand (shop)	老字号	lǎozìhào	名	35
long skirt	长裙	chángqún	名	39
look, observe	观	guān	动	40
lose	丢	diū	动	33
magazine	杂志	zázhì	名	31
main	主	zhǔ	形	40
make an enquiry	打听	dǎting	动	35
make public	公开	gōngkāi	动	36
Malaysia	马来西亚	Mǎláixīyà	专名	31
management	管理	guǎnlǐ	名/动	38
manner; approach	方式	fāngshì	名	32
mansion	府	fǔ	名	35

mark	标	biāo	名/动	33
mark	标记	biāojì	名	33
martial art	武术	wǔshù	名	32
mass	众	zhòng	名	38
mate	伙	huǒ	名	37
maths	数学	shùxué	名	31
meaning	意思	yìsi	名	31
member of a competition team	队员	duìyuán	名	32
memorial hall	纪念堂	jìniàntáng	名	40
meter, rice	米	mǐ	量/名	40
method	方法	fāngfǎ	名	36
military	武	wǔ	名/形	32
mind; manage	管	guǎn	动	33
mini skirt	超短裙	chāoduǎnqún	名	39
miss; study; read	念	niàn	动	34
mistake for	误以为	wù yǐwéi		37
mistake, wrong	错误	cuòwù	名	37
mixed	杂	zá	形	31
mode	模	mó	名	40
month	月份	yuèfen	名	34
most of	大部分	dàbùfen	形	32
mother	娘	niáng	名	39
mountain climb	爬山	pá shān	名/动	38
multiple	多元	duōyuán	形	37
museum	博物馆	bówùguǎn	名	40
must	必须	bìxū	情动	34
must	须	xū	情动	34
name	起名	qǐmíng	动/名	31
nationality	国籍	guójí	名	38
native town; record	籍	jí	名	38
necessary	必要	bìyào	形	39
next of kin; kiss	亲	qīn	形	37
no matter	不管	bùguǎn	连	33
North Star	紫微星	zǐwéixīng	专名	40
not necessarily	不见得	bújiànde	副	37
not only	不仅	bùjǐn	连	32
not only…but also…	不仅…而且	bùjǐn…érqiě		32
note	条	tiáo	名	36
noticc	通知	tōngzhī	名	36

notice; attention	注意	zhùyì	动/名	35
noun prefix	阿	ā		37
now	目前	mùqián	副	38
number	数	shù	名	31
occupy	占	zhàn	动	40
occupy an area of	占地	zhàndì	动	40
of; object substitute	之	zhī		35
office	办公室	bàngōngshì	名	31
old (not for age)	旧	jiù	形	33
on purpose; old	故	gù	副	39
on the spot	当场	dāngchǎng	副	39
one of	之一	zhī yī		35
oneself	己	jǐ	代	36
oneself	自己	zìjǐ	代	36
only	仅	jǐn	副	32
onomatopoeic character	乒	pīng	名	32
onomatopoeic character	乓	pāng	名	32
open lecture	讲座	jiǎngzuò	名	36
opposite, contrary;	相反	xiāngfǎn	形	37
opposite; against	反	fǎn	形	37
or	或	huò	连	34
or	或者	huòzhě	连	34
oral	口头	kǒutóu	形	36
orchid	兰	lán	名	38
ordinary; common	一般	yìbān	形	31
original	原	yuán	副	34
originally	原来	yuánlái	副	34
other, another	另	làng	副/代	33
otherwise, if not	不然	bùrán	连	31
outstanding	出色	chūsè	形	35
outstanding	出众	chūzhòng	形	38
overdraft	透支	tòuzhī	动/名	33
palace	宫	gōng	名	40
parcel	包裹	bāoguǒ	名	34
parcel; wrap	裹	guǒ	名/动	34
partner	伙伴	huǒbàn	名	37
pass on	传	chuán	动	38
paste	膏	gāo	名	39
pay	支	zhī	动	33

pay fees	交费	jiāo fèi	动	31
peaceful; arrange	安	ān	形/动	40
perfect; essence	精	jīng	形/名	38
period; session	节	jié	量	32
perm one's hair	烫发	tàngfà	动/名	35
permeate; transparent	透	tóu	动/形	33
person	士	shì	名	35
person who is interested	有意者	yǒuyìzhě		38
pin number	密码	mìmǎ	名	33
place; department	处	chù	名	33
place; place where something exists	所在	suǒzài	名	40
places of interest	景点	jǐngdiǎn	名	40
plaits, pigtail	辫	biàn	名	37
plaits, pigtail	辫子	biànzi	名	37
plank	板	bǎn	名	35
post	邮	yóu	名	34
post office	邮局	yóujú	名	34
preferential price	优惠价	yōuhuìjià	名	39
premier, prime minister	总理	zǒnglǐ	名	40
preserve	保存	bǎocún	动	40
pressing	急	jí	形	36
private, personal	私	sī	形	32
private, personal	私人	sīrén	形	32
procedure	手续	shǒuxù	名	31
products	制品	zhìpǐn	名	34
profession	职	zhí	名	33
promote; market	推销	tuīxiāo	动	38
pronunciation	语音	yǔyīn	名	37
public notice, announcement	通告	tōnggào	名	36
pull	拉	lā	动	36
purchase	购	gòu	动	39
push	推	tuī	动	38
put; hold	装	zhuāng	动	39
pyjama	睡衣	shuìyī	名	34
queue	排队	pái duì	动	35
queue; row	排	pái	动/名	35
quilt	被	bèi	名	34
quilt cover	被套	bèitào	名	34
rank	列	liè	名	33

rather…than…	与其…不如	yǔqí…bùrú	连	39
reach	达	dá	动	37
read	读	dú	动	31
read	阅	yuè	动	31
reading room	阅览室	yuèlǎnshì	名	31
ready-made	现成	xiànchéng	形	36
real son of the dragon (emperor)	真龙天子	zhēnlóng tiānzǐ	名	40
record	纪	jì	动	34
records	志	zhì	名	31
recruit	招聘	zhāopìn	动	38
refine	炼	liàn	动	32
register	挂号	guàhào	名/动	34
record, register	注	zhù	动	31
register	注册	zhùcè	动/名	31
relatively	比较	bǐjiào	副	33
repair; study	修	xiū	动	31
report one's arrival or presence	报到	bàodào	动	31
respect	尊	zūn	动	36
respect	尊敬	zūnjìng	名/动	36
rest assure of	放心	fàngxīn	形	33
return; satisfy	偿	cháng	动	34
reveal, show	显	xiǎn	动	35
risk	风险	fēnxiǎn	名	38
rite, ceremony	仪式	yíshì	名	40
roast lamb	羊肉	yángròu	名	36
robe	袍子	páozi	名	37
rostrum	城楼	chénglōu	名	40
royal family	皇家	huángjiā	名	38
royal palace	皇宫	huánggōng	名	40
rule	规	guī	名/动	34
salary	工资	gōngzī	名	38
salute	敬礼	jìnglǐ	名/动	36
scald, burn	烫	tàng	动	35
scale	规模	guīmó	名	40
scene	景	jǐng	名	40
scholarship	奖学金	jiǎngxuéjīn	名	33
school/college team	校队	xiàoduì	名	32
science (subjects of study)	理科	lǐkē	名	31
scientific name, formal name	学名	xuémíng	名	32

scope, range	范围	fànwéi	名	36
Scotland	苏格兰	Sūgélán	专名	38
seal; M.W for letter	封	fēng	动/量	37
seat	席	xí	名	40
secrecy, secret	密	mì	名/形	33
select	选	xuǎn	动	32
select an optional course	选修	xuǎnxiū	动/名	32
self-conscious	自觉	zìjué	形	32
sell	销	xiāo	动	38
send back, return, retreat	退	tuì	动	37
series; serial	系列	xìliè	名	33
set up	设	shè	动	31
settle (a transaction) by (a currency)	结算	jiěsuàn	名/动	33
share; m.w for a job or newspapers	份	fèn	名	33
sheet	单	dān	名	34
ship steamer	轮船	lúnchuán	名	34
short	短	duǎn	形	35
sign	签	qiān	动	36
single; bill	单	dān	形/名	33
site	址	zhǐ	名	33
situated at/in	位于	wèiyú	动	35
skill	技能	jìnéng	名	38
skill; technology	技	jì	名	38
small, tiny	微	wéi	形	40
smart	精	jīng	形	35
smart looking, spirit	精神	jīngshén	形/名	35
smart; handsome	帅	shuài	形	35
soap	肥皂	féizào	名	39
soap	皂	zào	名	39
soap with fragrance	香皂	xiāngzào	名	39
solar calendar; Gregory calendar	阳历	yánglì	名	34
special grade/class; superfine	特级	tèjí	形	35
spirit; god	神	shén	名	35
spoil; be used to	惯	guàn	动	37
square formed by cross lines; check	格	gé	名	31
square metre	平方米	píngfāngmǐ	名	40
stamp	邮票	yóupiào	名	34
start (business)	开业	kāiyè	动/名	35
starting point	起点	qǐdiǎn	名	31

steal	盗	dào	动	33
stipulation	规定	guīdìng	名/动	34
stop	停止	tíngzhǐ	动	40
stop	止	zhǐ	动	40
street	街	jiē	名	35
strength	力量	lìliàng	名	31
student card	学生证	xuéshēngzhèng	名	32
student union	学生会	xuéshēnghuì	名	36
stupid, slow	笨	bèn	形	36
style; shape; model	型	xíng	名	35
substitute; on behalf of	替	tì	动/介	36
suffix for person	者	zhě		38
Sun; masculine	阳	yáng	名	34
supermarket	超市	chāoshì	名	33
table of contents, catalogue	目录	mùlù	名	32
table tennis	乒乓球	pīngpāngqíu	名	32
take turns	轮	lún	动	35
talent	才	cái	名	38
talent	才华	cáihuá	名	38
talk	讲	jiǎng	动	36
team	队	duì	名	32
tell	告	gào	动	36
tell	告诉	gàosu	动	36
tell	诉	sù	动	36
ten thousand	万	wàn	数	39
that; particle	其	qí	代	39
The Great Hall of the People	人民大会堂	Rénmín Dàhuìtáng	专名	40
the youth	青年人	qíngniánrén	名	32
think; miss	思	sī	动	31
this, that	该	gāi	代	35
thus, therefore	因而	yīn'ér	连	40
Tian'anmen	天安门	Tiān'anmén	专名	40
tie; control	束	shù	动	40
tight	紧	jǐn	形	36
time calculation method	历法	lìfǎ	名	34
to	至	zhì	介	38
to colour	染	rǎn	动	35
to the end	到底	dàodǐ	副	34
tooth brush	牙刷	yáshuā	名	39

toothpaste	牙膏	yágāo	名	39
toward	往	wǎng	介	33
transport	输	shū	名/动	34
transport	运	yùn	动	34
transport by air	空运	kōngyùn	名	34
transport by sea	海运	hǎiyùn	名	34
transport; lose	运输	yùnshū	动	34
trousers (without padding)	单裤	dānkù	名	39
type; like	般	bān	名	31
uncle	伯	bó	名	37
unexpectedly	居然	jūrán	副	38
unit	元	yuán	名	33
unit; module	单元	dānyuán	名	33
up to now	至今	zhìjīn	副	38
urgent	紧急	jǐnjí	形	36
users; client	用户	yònghù	名	34
utilise; use	使用	shǐyòng	动	33
value insurance	保价	bǎojià	名	34
value; price	价	jià	名	34
vast, extensive	博	bó	形	40
very good (colloquial); bat, stick	棒	bàng	形/名	32
very much (colloquial)	不得了	bùdéliǎo	副	39
very much; a great deal	死去活来	sǐqù-huólái		39
visit; see	顾	gù	动	35
visit	访	fǎng	动	40
visit and tour around (a place)	参观	cānguān	动	40
volume, book	册	cè	名	31
walk about	逛	guàng	动	39
warm; welcome	热情	rèqíng	形	38
weigh; be called as; scale	称	chēng	动	34
well	井	jǐng	名	35
wheel	轮	lún	名	34
which, that	所	suǒ	助	40
which	何	hé	名	40
whole; complete	全	quán	形	37
win	胜	shèng	名/动	38
wish	祝	zhù	动	37
with	与	yǔ	连	39
with nicc and elegant appearance	美观大方	měiguān-dàfāng		39

Dr George Xinsheng Zhang is the Director of the Language Centre, School of Oriental and African Studies. He has over twenty years' experience working in British and Chinese universities with interest in language acquisition, cross cultural communications and teacher training. He was awarded professorship in language education by a Chinese university in 1994.

Linda Mingfang Li is a senior lecturer in Chinese and associate head of the Department of Languages and Cross Cultural Studies, Regent's College, London. She has taught English and Chinese in secondary, tertiary and higher education in China and the UK with interest in applied linguistics, social linguistics and language teaching for business purposes.

Dr William Xianfu Yu is a teacher of Chinese at SOAS language centre. He graduated from the Chinese department of Shanghai Teachers' College and the East China Normal University. He learnt Chinese in the department of Chinese Language and Literature in the two universities for eight years. He also obtained an MA degree in Linguistics, and a PH.D degree in Linguistics from University of London. He has 40 years experience in Chinese teaching. He was award a professorship in Chinese in China.

CHINESE IN STEPS

Appendices